Tradition History and the Old Testament

by
Walter E. Rast

Fortress Press

Fortress Press
Philadelphia

To My Parents

Library of Congress Catalog Card Number 70-171509

ISBN 0-8006-1460-7

Fifth Printing 1982

9713B82   Printed in the United States of America   1-1460

Editor's Foreword

The production of the Hebrew Bible was a long and complicated process. In all its stages, from beginning to end, it lasted well over a thousand years; and each attempt to describe it discloses more of its complexity.

Despite many changes in special aims and tasks, modern scholarship has persisted with great constancy in its intention of telling the story of how the Bible came to be. Its orientation has been historical and its efforts to describe the contents of the Old Testament and their history have developed three clearly distinguishable methods of study: literary criticism, form criticism, and tradition criticism. Each one of these is really a discipline in its own right. All are interested in the whole story; but each one constitutes a sort of crosscut attempt at giving its account of the whole. And so each one has developed its own techniques and methods of analysis, appropriate to the phenomena on which it concentrates.

Since they "dug in" at very different points in the complex legacy, and since they developed methods of scientific work as distinctive as their special tasks, these three disciplines sometimes give the impression of being arrayed against each other in mutually exclusive fashion. That is not the case; they are interrelated. All three want to contribute to the telling of one story. Their interrelationship is organic and logical. Each discipline lives off the questions that have baffled the other two. Since none of the three is able to ask or deal with all of the questions that must be asked and dealt with to tell the story of the making of the Old Testament, and since all want to tell that story, their relationships are complementary. It is thus fitting that these three small volumes, corresponding to the three disciplines of modern criticism, should appear under a single title, "Guides to Biblical Scholarship."

Literary criticism was the first on the scene. At the outset it was a special variation of textual study. Concentrating on the Book of Genesis, Astruc discovered a literary pattern related to the variant use of the divine names which led him to conclude that, in dealing with the era of the patriarchs, Moses had made use of more than one document or "source" in producing the first book of the Bible. There was an Elohist source and a Yahwist one. The variant use of the divine names came to an end in the third chapter of Exodus. However, using the characteristics of the sources discovered by means of it as criteria, scholars soon extended documentary source study into the entire Pentateuch, and to the Book of Isaiah!

With the movement that carries the name of Wellhausen, literary criticism took a new turn; having focused on the discovery of documentary sources and the marks of their identification, it now began to ask about the setting and motivation that had originally prompted the production of these separate units. One of the incidental by-products of this development was that literary criticism now often carried the popular name of "historical criticism," or "higher criticism," to differentiate it from textual criticism which was "lower!" Of more profound significance for our understanding of the meaning of the whole story was the fact that this movement assumed that the production of Scripture was conditioned historically not only by the fact that it had combined documents with a prior history of their own, but also that wider movements in human life had influenced their contents. Implicit questions about revelation and the inspiration of Scripture were made more pressing.

Historical criticism complicated the questions about documentary sources raised by the earlier phase of literary criticism; but it could not deal with them. For example, though there was general agreement that the Pentateuch combined four sources, there was no unanimity about precisely what belonged to each of these. More serious still were the disagreements about the antecedent history of each of the four. Did each combine two or more separate units? And could one detect the hand of the redactor who had combined them? Or was each of the four strands a single unit that had gone through several stages of annotation and editing? And how large a role had been played by the final redactor(s) who had given the Pentateuch or the Book of Isaiah their present forms? The riddles were growing in number and the frustration they produced called for a new beginning. It was in this context that form criticism arose.

In his famous essay, "The Problem of the Hexateuch," written in the thirties, G. von Rad tells how the old methods of literary criticism failed to deal with his questions. In his frustration the rubrics for the presentation of the offering of first fruits caught his attention. This text (Deuteronomy 26:1–11) was one of the relatively few in which the prescriptions for what is to be done in a situation are combined with the words to be recited. It was the form of the recital—an enumeration of the acts of God in Israel's history—that von Rad found most important; he called it a *Credo*, and he proceeded to build his interpretation of all of Israel's traditions around this form. Gunkel and Mowinckel were pioneers in form criticism who preceded von Rad; but what is striking about the case of von Rad is how the limitations of literary criticism landed him in form criticism.

Form criticism concentrates on primary categories of form rather than on documents: the hymn, the blessing, the legend, the lament, and many, many more. That is its most original contribution. It combines this concentration with the historical interest in setting and function first stressed by the historical critics of Wellhausen's day. Who used a given form? in what context? and for what purposes? Form criticism depends greatly on the results of research in such areas as cult and liturgy, social psychology, and anthropology, for the meaning of a given unit depends as much on its function in the life of the community as on the positive contents of its form. Indeed, many form critics would insist that this *Sitz im Leben* is of far greater importance than contents for our understanding; and all would probably agree that it is indispensable.

The internal tensions and bifurcations in the practice of form criticism parallel those we have noted in literary criticism. There a study of the documents themselves competed with an interest in describing the social and political scene in which they were written. Here the analysis of the forms and the exposition of their contents is crowded by a desire to describe the character and significance of the ceremonial that originally developed them. This distinction is classically illustrated by two pioneers in the form critical movement, Hermann Gunkel and his pupil, Sigmund Mowinckel. Both concentrated most of their work on the Book of Psalms. Gunkel assumed psalms were essentially personal and private compositions, even when produced to express a public or communal mood. Though he recognized that their forms were shaped in ancient cultic settings, he was less preoccupied with those settings and their role than with the thought of the authors of psalms. Mowinckel reversed the focus. He became a historian of religion and cult, assuming that psalms had been written for the sake of their role in the actual ceremonial of worship rather than simply for the sake of expressing the experience of an individual author. Mowinckel himself expressed the distinction in the original Norwegian title of his great work, *The Psalms in Israel's Worship*. He called it *Offersang og Sangoffer*, which can be translated "Song of sacrifice and Sacrifice of song." Gunkel had stressed the latter; the song was the thing. Mowinckel emphasized the former; the liturgy which the song was to serve.

Literary criticism dealt with units of the Bible, and with the historical settings in which tthe writing occurred. Form criticism deals with an earlier preliterary phase of the story. At that stage Israel made its public witness to its understanding of itself in its relation to God in a wide variety of fixed forms suited to oral communication: blessings, oaths, hymns, legends, commandments, and many, many more. Eventually the forms became imbedded in Israel's literature. The process of self-definition which was so productive of what eventually became literary forms, took place in an almost endless variety of circumstances in relation to the family, the temple, the school, the courts, the realm of the state and diplomacy, commerce

vi

and trade—to name some of the primary orbits. Sometimes a specific act of this endless process of self-definition involved only a single Israelite. In other instances many persons or recognized groups participated in this process. Very often, too, the whole community of Israel expressed itself in these specific occasions that gave shape to and confirmed the use of particular forms.

Form criticism presupposes that, however unwittingly, all Israelites over many centuries contributed to the making of the Bible; that it was simply a result of their having had a communal existence as Israelites. The interest and intention of form criticism is analytical; it concentrates on detailed aspects of the common life and on the specific forms nurtured by them. There is an interest in the pristine structure of such forms which views all subsequent elaboration or mixing of forms in larger units as a sort of secondary development. There is less interest in telling the story of the making of the Bible as a whole than in describing separately a great number of "scenes" that are finally to be absorbed by that story. Form criticism does not really answer the questions of literary criticism about the editing and combining of documentary units. It puts them in parentheses while going behind them to an earlier stage in the process. There it discloses scenes in the history of the making of the Bible hitherto unknown, scenes in which the practices of common life rather than writing are conspicuous. Thus, for the time being, the unanswered questions left by literary criticism are relativized in their importance, and left untouched. But eventually they reassert themselves, for analysis of primary scenes alone is not capable of telling the story.

Tradition criticism—in New Testament studies the preferred term is "redaction criticism"—responds to a new urge to tell the whole story. Its intentions are synthetic and presuppose the analytic work of both literary and form criticism. Since it follows in the wake of both, it assumes that both oral and written continuities play a role in the shaping of the traditions that finally culminated in Scripture. Individual historians of tradition will vary with respect to the emphasis they place upon one or the other. A comparison of the work of Martin

Noth with that of Ivan Engnell illustrates this variation rather well. More significant, perhaps, than their differences in approach and method—or in results—is the fact that both presuppose and use the results of the efforts of literary and form criticism. The proportional significance assigned to oral and written means of transmission, respectively, is a minor matter compared to the common recognition that the whole community, in all expressions of its existence, participated in giving shape to the tradition and in handing it on, generation after generation.

Form criticism concentrates on primary forms—on the beginnings of the shaping of the traditions that finally result in the Old Testament. Redaction criticism, as distinct from tradition history, deals with the very last stages of the editing that presents Scripture in its fixed or final form. Tradition criticism is interested in all the stages that lie in between form and redaction criticism, the history of a tradition which, in the Old Testament, spans more than a millennium. In New Testament studies, which deal in a time span less than a tenth as long, there is an understandable tendency to conflate the study of tradition with that of the final process of editing. The situation is very different with respect to the Old Testament where the history of tradition contains so many facets and stages, all of which can by no means be described as "redactional." Form criticism helps to make us aware of that.

Literary criticism tried to tell the story of the making of the Bible as a story of writing and editing. At the crest of its influence it had asked a great many questions about the history of this process which it found unanswerable on the basis of literary presuppositions alone. Form criticism introduced the presupposition that the making and transmission of the contents of the Bible had an oral as well as a written side to it. This has given tradition critics the sort of freedom and flexibility which literary criticism lacked, and from the lack of which it suffered. This freedom has resulted in promising new essays. As an example, one may refer to Martin Noth's proposal. He suggests that there was a Deuteronomic Historian, a single personality, who made use of all of the older materials contained in that part of the Old Testament that begins with Deuteronomy and ends with 2 Kings. This proposal was Noth's way of getting across some quite specific and personal notions about the meaning of Israel's history. Making this proposal depends on the sort of awareness of openness and freedom made possible by form criticism. Literary criticism had always contemplated the tying together of the material in these books as a process carried on by a series of "Deuteronomic editors," conforming to the notion that the growth of tradition was by a process of writing, only. Noth's imagination and skill as a historian of tradition who presupposes a more open situation because of the oral character of much in the tradition enable him to endow this large section of the Old Testament with a freshness, a pointed clarity, and a unity such as it never had before.

It becomes increasingly clear that the three disciplines featured in this series are interdependent, as well as distinct. They all want to tell the same story; and they need each other's help in doing so. And they can help each other because, as we said at the outset, the orientation of all three is historical.

The historicality of the Bible, that is, the conditioned character of its contents, a conditioned-ness which makes them dependent upon all kinds of human limitations and situations in precisely the same way as the legacies of all sorts of historical traditions, is an assumption of modern criticism throughout. That assumption makes it modern. At the outset the assumption was held very tentatively, even fearfully, and in relatively circumscribed fashion. It asserted itself in the face of venerable traditions of dogma and confessional authority that equated the form of the contents of Scripture, its verbal conceptualizations, with the divine absolute. But the assumptions so gingerly held at the outset were to vindicate their tenability and importance in the process. The Bible is a far more historical book than the pioneers of historical criticism ever dreamed; and we are aware of this precisely because what they began continued: from literary criticism, to form criticism, to tradition criticism. In one way or another, over a period of more than a thousand years, the whole cultural setting of the ancient world of the Near East and every Israelite in all those centuries had some sort of a hand in the making of the Bible.

Needless to say, the impact of these developments on theology has been tremendous and continues as a powerful influence today. The word of God in relation to Scripture, as well as in relation to the church and the world, is being redefined and conceptualized in dynamic, fresh ways today because of the theological implications of modern criticism. Criticism set out to tell the story of the Bible. It did not intend to deal with theology, let alone launch new movements in theology. Nevertheless, however unintentionally, it did both.

J. COERT RYLAARSDAM

Contents

Preface

A word of appreciation is due the following who have contributed in one way or another to the content and form of this book: members of a biblical seminar at Valparaiso University during 1968, who participated with me in discussing problems of traditio-historical interpretation; and colleagues in the Department of Theology at the same institution, who offered valuable insights in a series of staff meetings devoted to the implications of Gerhard von Rad's work on Old Testament theology. I am also grateful to Ruth Pullmann for typing the manuscript, and to the Committee on Creative Work and Research of Valparaiso University for assistance in working on this study, and others, during the year 1970–71.

WALTER E. RAST

I

The Transmission of
Old Testament Traditions

The method called "tradition history" in Old Testament studies today developed not so much independently as in correlation with other discoveries. Studies in the area of form criticism contributed to its emergence, as did those in the "history of religions." So also did new data from the ancient Near Eastern world brought to light by archaeology. Each of these newer materials and perceptions in its own way led students of the Old Testament to take more seriously the setting of the ancient world in which the Old Testament was produced, and to examine anew its formation in the light of that world. This kind of study has been of incalculable value in recovering the message of the Old Testament for our own time. But it has also forced us to see how different that world was from our own in nearly every respect, including its way of producing literature.

When we today use the word "literature" we usually think of a novel, a collection of poems, or a work of history—all printed in book form by a modern printing firm. The people of the ancient Near East, on the other hand, would have had a broader and different meaning for the same term. The Old Testament might refer to a "book" (*sēpher*), as the Book of Deuteronomy does (Deut. 17:18; 28:58), but it would certainly have had a different conception of what is meant by that term than we. For the Old Testament people, the concept of a book would have included, in addition to written pieces, the consciousness of something which had been passed on for generations beforehand, often by word of mouth. And in any concept of "literary figures," the ancients would have thought not only of writers, but also of gifted people who could call to mind episodes about renowned persons and events, and who could sometimes spontaneously rhapsodize on the meaning of significant events. That is, the understanding of literature included various elements which do not belong to our experience in a more book-conscious culture.

One thing that this kind of study has brought to light is the widespread use of oral tradition by the peoples of the ancient Near East. Although the role of this phenomenon should not be overestimated, it has many ramifications for the interpretation of the Old Testament. The traditio-historical method of biblical study has been spurred on by this growing acquaintance with oral tradition in the ancient world, and this discovery has led to an intricate examination of the types of literary transmission involved in the production of the Old Testament.

HERMANN GUNKEL AND ORAL TRADITION

While an Old Testament scholar like Richard Simon had already in the seventeenth century recognized the importance of tradition in the formation of the Old Testament, it remained for Hermann Gunkel (1862–1932) to pursue the full implications of this insight.[1] Although Gunkel is remembered primarily for his pioneering efforts in form criticism, he made contributions to many areas of the study of the Old Testament. This great versatility in his work, which has led to enduring contributions, has moved W. F. Albright to describe Gunkel as "one of the most remarkable Old Testament scholars of modern times."[2]

1. For treatments of Simon's life and work, see Hans-Joachim Kraus, *Geschichte der historisch-kritischen Erforschung des Alten Testaments* (Neukirchen: Buchhandlung des Erziehungsvereins, 1956), pp. 59–64, and Jean Steinmann, "Biblical Criticism," *Twentieth Century Encyclopedia of Catholicism*, vol. 63 (New York: Hawthorne Books, 1958), pp. 46–48.

2. In the Introduction to Hermann Gunkel, *The Legends of Genesis: The Biblical Saga and History*, trans. W. H. Carruth (New York: Schocken Books, 1964), p. vii. This English translation contains the initial part of Gunkel's commentary on Genesis.

2

As a student of Old Testament literature, Gunkel gave special attention to problems in the formation of that literature. In this regard, he can be compared with his great contemporary, Julius Wellhausen. During the latter part of the nineteenth century, Wellhausen had largely gained preeminence in the field of Old Testament studies with his remarkable reconstruction of Israel's history, based on the combined results of documentary criticism.[3] However, Wellhausen's presentation, brilliant though it was, suffered from some severe limitations. As a documentary critic Wellhausen's interest was chiefly in "sources," which he interpreted principally as written documents, and to which he ascribed the primary creative impulses in the formation of the religion of Israel. This does not mean that he failed to recognize older material in the sources, for the concept of tradition was important in his work.[4] But he was reluctant, for example, to recognize much of anything of the patriarchal traditions of the Book of Genesis as antedating the time of David.[5] Gunkel, on the other hand, may be said to have opened up further perspectives in that he comprehended a stage in the history of the Old Testament literature during which literary formation was often influenced by means of oral communication. Along with his form analysis of differing types of literature such as songs, fables, and saga, he was able to push behind the sources of the documentary critics to earlier units of tradition. Gunkel's studies thus delivered a challenge to the widely accepted interpretation received from Wellhausen.

Of all Gunkel's contributions, his work on the dynamics of oral tradition in the ancient Near Eastern world is, perhaps, most decisive. We can see his usage of this principle, for example, in the first part of his famous commentary on Genesis.[6] Here Gunkel dealt with the numerous questions which arise concerning the nature of the literature in the

3. Julius Wellhausen, *Prolegomena to the History of Ancient Israel* (Cleveland: World Meridian Books, 1961). First published in German in 1878.
4. It is interesting that "History of Tradition" supplies the title for Part 2 of Wellhausen's work.
5. Wellhausen, *Prolegomena*, p. 322.
6. Gunkel, *The Legends of Genesis.*

Book of Genesis. Introducing the special term "saga," he discussed the role of popular tradition in the formation of the material in the Book of Genesis. According to his view, the composition of the Book of Genesis came about in a number of complex stages. The book, as we now have it, represents only the last step in the long process of its formation. Behind this final stage one can discern an earlier time during which a number of independent sagas have come to be amalgamated. Usually these sagas have already been reworked into prose versions by the time they have been incorporated into a larger narrative. But at a still earlier period individual sagas, such as we have in great abundance in the different stories of the patriarchal narratives, were transmitted in poetic form and by means of oral tradition. Of particular significance here is Gunkel's contention that this early stage of oral transmission had a creative impact on the formation of the tradition which was passed on.[7]

Gunkel's influence, then, has provided the stimulus not only for the impressive studies in form criticism which have continued during this century, but also for the developing interest in the history of transmission of the Old Testament literature. His emphasis on the role of oral tradition as well as his work on the various stages in the composition of the Old Testament literature, have been crucial for subsequent efforts. The latter also anticipated some of the recent procedures of "redaction criticism," which attempts to examine the way older traditions have been utilized by the redactor(s) in the last, important stages of composition.

A final observation on Gunkel's legacy to Old Testament study should be made—one which will lead us directly into the discussion of the methods at the present. This is the strong interest that Gunkel had in the comparative literature of the ancient Near East, an interest generated along with his study of "the history of religions." Gunkel participated in the concerns of the so-called history of religions school, which had become prominent by the end of the nineteenth century. These contacts led him to stress the importance of considering comparative evidence in studying the Old Testament, just

7. Ibid., pp. 88–122.

as his interests were also drawn to the increasing amount of archaeological material coming from the Middle East. Thus, when Gunkel examined the nature of Israelite tradition, he did so with the assistance of this growing body of comparative material from the ancient world. Such material helps to clarify some important questions as to how literature was composed and transmitted in the world of the ancient Near East. It will be helpful at this point to consider several illustrations of how materials of this kind may illuminate the processes of transmission in the Old Testament.

TRANSMISSION OF LITERATURE IN THE ANCIENT WORLD

Like the literature of the Old Testament, some of the literary remains of other ancient peoples also passed through an oral stage prior to the point at which the traditions were fixed in writing. An interesting analogy to the composition of the Old Testament, for example, is found in a literature from an entirely different setting, the Homeric epics. Although much remains to be solved regarding the complex problems of composition in these epics, classicists are more and more inclined to visualize a period of oral transmission in pre-Homeric times during which a significant organization of the epic cycles was already occurring.[8] While the content of these Greek epic cycles differs from that of the biblical literature, the process of transmission, the role of oral tradition, and the use of stock formulae characteristic of epic style, provide interesting parallels to similar features in parts of the Old Testament.

An example much closer to the world of the Old Testament itself is the well-known Epic of Gilgamesh.[9] In this piece of literature we possess the remains of an epic series that was widely disseminated in old Babylonia, and even before that,

8. See on this Albert B. Lord, *The Singer of Tales*, Harvard Studies in Comparative Literature, no. 24 (Cambridge: Harvard University Press, 1960).

9. A reliable study is still that of Alexander Heidel, *The Gilgamesh Epic and Old Testament Parallels* (Chicago: University of Chicago, Phoenix Books, 1946).

in Sumeria, with which its earliest stages are to be identified. The history of the transmission of this literature is significant for students of the Old Testament since it provides information and background on the processes involved in the compilation of literature in the ancient Near Eastern world.

We know the Gilgamesh Epic from relatively late texts, written in the Akkadian language during the seventh century B.C. They were discovered about the middle of the last century at Nineveh in the ruins of the temple library of the Assyrian king, Ashurbanipal.[10] Several older fragments of the epic were subsequently discovered at Boghazköy, the capital of the ancient Hittite Empire, and these remnants included both a Hittite and Hurrian translation. The oldest extant texts are in Old Babylonian, and go back to the first half of the second millennium, but even these evidently represent copies of earlier texts. The probable date of the epic in the form we now have it, then, is about the turn of the second millennium.[11] Concerning this ancient epic, Alexander Heidel says: "The date of the composition of the Gilgamesh Epic can therefore be fixed at about 2000 B.C. But the material contained on these tablets is undoubtedly much older, as we can infer from the mere fact that the epic consists of numerous originally independent episodes, which, of course, did not spring into existence at the time of the composition of our poem but must have been current long before they were compiled and woven together to form our epic."[12]

Although Heidel does not discuss these problems in detail, his remarks suggest that the study of a work like this opens up certain problems of literary transmission which may not be unlike those of some parts of the Old Testament literature. His statements leave open the question of a possible role for oral transmission at early stages in the formation of the epic. Above all, they show how these originally independent cycles were coordinated into the larger epic itself in a process reminis-

10. Ibid., p. 1; see also the introductory notes of E. A. Speiser in *Ancient Near Eastern Texts Relating to the Old Testament*, ed. James B. Pritchard, 2d ed. (Princeton, N.J.: Princeton University Press, 1955), pp. 72–73.

11. Heidel, *The Gilgamesh Epic*, p. 15.

12. Ibid.

cent of final redactoral work in Old Testament composition.[13]

Tablet XI of the epic, the famous episode containing parallels to the flood narrative of the Old Testament, indicates how broad some of the problems raised by Old Testament traditiohistorical research can become, especially when materials from outside the Old Testament are also taken into account. The sources in Genesis 6–9 which documentary criticism concluded were essentially P and J material, show a distinct relation to the older Mesopotamian epic.[14] Yet, it is too facile to conclude, as has sometimes been done, that we possess here a simple case of borrowing. The differences in underlying viewpoint, as well as in many details, are too striking for oversimplified explanations. Here a perspective which takes into account the complexity of the formation of certain traditions, and their transmission, even across cultural and religious lines, can help to illuminate the history and meaning of a complicated text like the flood narrative. The fundamental question is: Through what processes have these Mesopotamian traditions come to be appropriated by the Israelites? There seems to be increasing evidence to support the view that the transmission of these traditions occurred through an intermediate group. Speiser, for example, has suggested that a northwesterly group may have played such a role.[15] Since the patriarchal traditions place the homeland of the ancestors of Israel in the region of upper Mesopotamia around Haran, and since this was a center not only of Hurrian but also Aramaean activity, it may be that the incorporation of these traditions into Israelite faith goes back ultimately to early contacts with peoples such as these.

What we have observed in these several cases, then, is that ancient literature outside the Old Testament provides illustrations of the complex processes through which certain types of literature passed before they came into their final form. Often this presupposes a period in which oral transmission is of

13. See A. Leo Oppenheim, *Ancient Mesopotamia: Portrait of a Dead Civilization* (Chicago: University of Chicago Press, 1964), pp. 252–62, for a further treatment of this epic, emphasizing the problems of its written form.
14. E. A. Speiser, *Genesis,* The Anchor Bible, vol. 1 (Garden City: Doubleday & Co., 1964), p. 55.
15. Ibid.

significance, although in some cases a written version of an oral tradition may have existed side by side with the former.[16] In any event, this newer data on literary composition in the ancient Near East, especially the role of oral tradition, has opened up a concern with the dynamics involved in this kind of transmission. This has also included an interest in the way memory and the poetic medium were important for such transmission.

MEMORY, POETRY, AND TRADITION

When it comes to memory, students of the Near East, ancient and modern, like to call attention to the great differences between that part of the world and our own. While in our society we have become accustomed to having things remembered for us, in books and written collections, and now in computers, people of the Near East have carried along a tradition in which the exercise of memory has been paramount. Even with the rapid change which that area is experiencing today, it is still possible to find people who are able to deliver large parts of such literature as the Koran from memory.

This practice is a vestige of what must have been a widely employed mode of transmission in the ancient world. In the world of the ancient Near East, writing and literacy were confined to a privileged few, scribes or royal archivists of more aristocratic background.[17] The common man, among whom at least the Old Testament literature would have found an audience, was usually not able to read or write. While we know from the Old Testament that trained people like scribes were important in the formation of the Israelite literature (Jer. 36: 1–8), we also have to allow for the place that ordinary people must have had in bringing the Old Testament traditions into being. In either case, however, there seems little reason to doubt that if memory is taken seriously for its role in the transmission of Old Testament traditions, then it is to be seen

16. William F. Albright, *From the Stone Age to Christianity*, 2d ed. (Garden City: Doubleday Anchor Books, 1957), p. 64.
17. Edward Chiera, *They Wrote on Clay* (Chicago: University of Chicago Press, 1938), pp. 165–75.

8

not only as a marginal matter, but also as having had a deep effect upon the shape and character of the message itself.[18]

Along with the function of memory in the world of the Old Testament, there has arisen an accompanying interest in poetry as facilitating the exercise of memory. The numerous formulae, along with the parallelism and wordplay so characteristic of ancient Near Eastern as well as Old Testament poetry, all point to the importance that this mode played in the preservation of traditions. Those responsible for the perpetuation of certain memories would have found the medium of poetry the most congenial for recalling these traditions. In the Old Testament, the patriarchal traditions seemingly passed through such a period when they were found essentially in poetic form, and occasionally vestiges of such an earlier form still appear, fossillike, in the later prose versions.[19] The fact that the prophetic books are also largely collections of poetic oracles points back to the widespread use of the same medium for this literature. All of which is not to suggest that there was no usage of prose in earlier times, for clearly that form could also be employed. The point is that poetry provided a special adaptability for times when oral transmission was prevalent.

ORAL TRADITION IN SCANDINAVIAN SCHOLARSHIP

The pivot for much of the discussion about oral tradition is found in the work of a number of Scandinavian scholars, who have raised in a special way the problem of the relation between oral and written transmission in the Old Testament literature. The scholar who launched this discussion was H. S. Nyberg, in a study of the Book of Hosea published in 1935.[20] In this significant study, Nyberg suggested for the first time a far-reaching principle for the study of the Old Testament as a whole. Utilizing the results of the study of oral tradition in the Old Testament up to that time, he advanced the revolution-

18. See the study of Brevard S. Childs, *Memory and Tradition in Israel*, Studies in Biblical Theology, no. 37 (Naperville, Ill.: Alec R. Allenson, 1962).
19. See the recent remarks of William F. Albright, *Yahweh and the Gods of Canaan* (Garden City: Doubleday & Co., 1968), pp. 50–52.
20. H. S. Nyberg, *Studien zum Hoseabuche* (Uppsala: Lundequistska, 1935).

9

izing thesis that the bulk of Old Testament literature was shaped and transmitted orally until the crisis of the exilic period. Only at this time did the conditions occur which necessitated the writing down of the literature. Nyberg amassed an impressive amount of evidence to support this basic thesis, beginning with text critical questions and solutions, and working on to his broader conclusions.

Nyberg's work furnished one of the basic ingredients for much of the subsequent study of the questions of tradition history carried out by scholars, especially in the Nordic countries. The new element in his work was the emphasis it placed for the first time on the priority of oral tradition in the composition of the Old Testament literature. The recognition of this means of transmission, Nyberg argued, must not be seen simply as an additional observation about the Old Testament literature. It must rather be viewed as a cardinal principle affecting methodology. Tradition history which takes into account this importance of oral transmission must be employed, therefore, as an analytic method. Such an outlook has led several scholars to abandon the older "source criticism" as a viable method. These latter have proposed that the traditio-historical method which they represent is a radically different method, in no way less critical than source criticism had attempted to be, but more integral to the Old Testament's own processes of formation.[21]

The most controversial, and probably the best-known, tradition historian among the Scandinavians was Ivan Engnell (1906-1964). Prior to his untimely death, Engnell taught at Uppsala and was a leading light in what has come to be called the "Uppsala School" of Old Testament studies. Although better known for his much debated views on divine kingship in the ancient Near East, his more enduring contributions will probably turn out to be his frequent discussions of methodology in approaching the Old Testament. The fact that some of his most important essays were produced in Swedish, and for years could only be read in that language, may account for the fact that his work has sometimes not been

21. Cf. Eduard Nielsen, *Oral Tradition*, Studies in Biblical Theology, no. 11 (Naperville, Ill.: Alec R. Allenson, 1954), pp. 11–17.

treated with as much candor as it ought.[22] For our purposes, his volume on introduction to the Old Testament, as well as a number of monographs and scattered articles devoted to his views of traditio historical research, are of special importance.[23]

Engnell adopted the conclusions of Nyberg on the importance of oral transmission, while stating repeatedly his great resistance to the methods of documentary criticism. From his perspective the latter were conditioned by a Western outlook which could only falsify the character and interpretation of the Old Testament. He contended that no written sources such as J and E ever existed, as the source critics of the Pentateuch thought of them. Nor did the process of composition occur, as they believed, by means of essentially written collections, additions, duplications, interpolations, and redactions. Rather, he held that the Old Testament literature was produced and circulated by groups of people concerned with preserving and developing certain traditions, and that this was done through long periods of oral transmission. In fact most of the questions of the composition of the Old Testament have to do with oral tradition, which had the most formative role in the production of that literature.[24]

Engnell's viewpoints on the question of transmission are evident wherever he devoted himself to discussions of the Old Testament material. As an illustration, we confine ourselves here simply to his important work on the D history, including the books of Deuteronomy through 2 Kings. In contrast to source criticism, which attempted to follow the four strands, J, E, D, and P, into these historical books, Engnell was led to the view that the dominant tradition given expression throughout these books was simply D. Subsequently, like Martin Noth's independent but similar view, he employed the

22. A selection of articles by Ivan Engnell has recently been translated into English by John T. Willis and published as *A Rigid Scrutiny* (Nashville: Vanderbilt University Press, 1969).
23. See his "Methodological Aspects of Old Testament Study," Supplements Vetus Testamentum 7 (1960), pp. 13–30.
24. C. R. North, "Pentateuchal Criticism," in *The Old Testament and Modern Study*, ed. H. H. Rowley (Oxford: Oxford Paperbacks, 1961), p. 65.

designation Deuteronomic History for these books. However, in contrast to Noth, Engnell was inclined to think more in terms of circles or groups of traditionists who were responsible for the production of this literature. These circles were viewed as continuing across many generations, during which time the traditions came into being, and were assembled into larger collections, until the amalgamation process eventuated in the large corpus we now possess. Again, the role of oral tradition was important, since we must assume that the essential features of the D tradition were arrived at during periods when such methods of transmission were widely in vogue.[25]

Engnell's discussion of transmission problems in the prophetic literature follows a similar line of attack.[26] As in the case of the historical traditions, he conceived of much of the prophetic literature as having moved from a stage of oral preaching to that of written form. This differed, however, in the case of different types of prophetic literature, which he termed the "liturgical" and "divan" types. The first he held to be a prophetic writing modeled on certain formal characteristics known from the cultic practices and forms of Israel. A prophetic work like the Book of Nahum belonged to this type, and its writing probably occurred at once. The second type, which Engnell called the divan type, consisted of those prophetic books which were built up of collections of the words of a prophet. These latter collection-type books must have experienced a considerable period of oral transmission prior to the time they were reduced to writing. During this period their disciples would have collected and expanded their words until they arrived in the form in which we now possess them.

It should be noted that this is only a cursory treatment of Engnell's frequent and involved methodological remarks. What is apparent is the large role that oral transmission is assumed to have played in the formation of various types of

25. For a brief account of Engnell's work on the D history, see North, "Pentateuchal Criticism," pp. 69–70.

26. For Engnell's views on the prophetic books see A *Rigid Scrutiny*, chapter 6.

Old Testament literature. At the same time, Engnell emphasized the necessity of studying the dynamics of the transmission of traditions in the widest context possible. He stressed
the importance of understanding the sociology of ancient
Israel. He took seriously the ancient Near Eastern milieu in
which Israel lived and encouraged an understanding of the
laws of oral tradition in terms of the ancient Near Eastern
peoples. Only in this way, he contended, would it be possible
to understand the ancient literature without certain modern
preconceptions, which could also lead to misconceptions.

Other Scandinavian scholars who have taken up the discussion of oral tradition, concentrating especially on the prophets,
are Harris Birkeland and Sigmund Mowinckel.[27] But the viewpoint is, perhaps, most accessible to English readers in Eduard
Nielsen's monograph on the subject.[28] Nielsen stressed the
importance of Nyberg's hypothesis that the writing of the Old
Testament literature was largely related to the crisis of the
exile, a time when the written preservation of traditions
became an unquestioned necessity. Although observing that
oral and written transmission should not be set up against
each other, at the same time he adopted a stance similar to
that of Engnell in viewing traditio-historical method not
simply as an addendum to earlier interpretation but rather as
a necessary alternative. Like Engnell, he rejected the usual
procedures of documentary criticism as applied to the Pentateuch and extrapolated to other Old Testament literature.

While these scholars have shared a common approach to
the problems of oral tradition—even though there may be
individual differences among them—one Scandinavian scholar
of the Old Testament and the ancient Near East has challenged this basic presentation. In a study of the phenomena
of transmission in the ancient Near East and the Old Testament, G. Widengren has argued that the efforts which stress
oral tradition in this fashion are based on a fundamental mis-

27. Harris Birkeland, *Zum hebräischen Traditionswesen* (Oslo: Jacob
Dybwad, 1958); Sigmund Mowinckel, *Prophecy and Tradition* (Oslo:
Jacob Dybwad, 1946).

28. Nielsen, *Oral Tradition*.

13

understanding.[29] Widengren joined others who had become dubious about the emphatic claims that were made for oral as against written transmission, pointing to the role that writing played very early among various peoples of the ancient Near East, such as the Phoenicians. Utilizing parallels from Arabic literature, he tried to establish the complementarity of oral and written transmission, which he saw as having been carried on side by side. Although several of his colleagues whom he criticized have argued in return that they did not intend to set up these two against one another, a certain ambiguity in the relation of the two types of transmission seems to be present in their work.[30]

THE DEBATE OVER ORAL VS. WRITTEN TRANSMISSION

The vigorous discussion about oral tradition in the Scandinavian countries was bound to arouse response from scholars in other countries. The question is significant enough for one's presuppositions in interpreting the Old Testament literature to warrant considerable discussion of the problem in itself. In general, the emphasis of Engnell, Nielsen, and others, has been considered to be an exaggeration, although the basic insight is held to be a valid one. In a monograph published in 1959, Antonius Gunneweg contended that, although oral tradition is the common means of transmission in the Old Testament as in the ancient Near East, at the same time there are many instances of writing before the exile. He notes that written scrolls were not unknown in the age of the prophets as well.[31]

The historian and archaeologist, Roland de Vaux, has also expressed himself against a one-sided emphasis on oral tradition. He cites as evidence various written documents now known to have originated in the Mesopotamian and Syro-Phoenician regions in very early times, as well as references in the Old Testament itself to such ancient writings as the Book of the Wars of Yahweh (Num. 21:14) or the Book of Yashar

29. G. Widengren, *Literary and Psychological Aspects of the Hebrew Prophets* (Uppsala: Lundequistska, 1948).
30. Cf. Nielsen, *Oral Tradition*, pp. 16–17.
31. Antonius H. J. Gunneweg, *Mündliche und schriftliche Tradition der vorexilischen Prophetenbücher als Problem der neueren Prophetenforschung* (Göttingen: Vandenhoeck & Ruprecht, 1959), pp. 40–41.

(Josh. 10:13; 2 Sam. 1:18).[32] In addition to these, there are now inscriptions which have been found at a number of Palestinian sites, and these show that the Canaanite alphabetic script was known in Palestine during the period of 1200 to 900 B.C., that is, during the period when some of the early Israelite tradition was taking shape.[33] However, Nyberg had attempted to counter this argument by insisting that these inscriptions are usually administrative tablets which bear no resemblance to the kind of literature found in the Old Testament. Thus, he concluded that writing in Palestine during the Iron Age was largely confined to business transactions, whereas epic and religious literature was essentially passed on by means of oral expression.[34]

The matter is not easily resolved, however, for those on either side of the debate. It is noteworthy, for example, how Nielsen tried to bring clarity to his position on this difficult question. On the one hand, he stressed that the primary mode of Old Testament transmission was oral. At the same time, he argued that this does not exclude the fact that sometimes a version of a tradition may have been written down, mostly out of a motive to aid the memory in the oral recitation of the tradition. However, the important fact is that this writing process had no formative influence on the actual composition since the latter received its shape largely in a period when the laws of oral transmission were in full force.[35]

It is evident, then, that just at this point various schools of Old Testament scholars today are divided. It seems likely, however, that Old Testament research of the future will not necessarily be tied to a rigid choice between these two forms of transmission. Rather, it is more probable that such study will attempt to understand the Old Testament material with the aid of comparative and internal data dealing with oral transmission, and it will find that this will sometimes put it

32. Roland de Vaux, "Reflexions sur l'État actuel de la critique du Pentateuque," in *Bible et Orient* (Paris: Les Éditions du Cerf, 1968), pp. 46–47.

33. Albright, *From the Stone Age to Christianity*, p. 75.

34. Nyberg, *Studien zum Hoseabuche*, pp. 7–8; see also Nielsen, *Oral Tradition*, pp. 24–25.

35. Nielsen, *Oral Tradition*, pp. 34–37.

into touch with the earliest levels of biblical tradition. At the same time, traditio-historical method will carry on its investigation into the more complex stages of the shaping of the traditions, as they are incorporated into larger cycles and eventually "histories" or "collections." This latter brings such investigation into close association with what is now called "redaction criticism," and at this stage it will find itself engaged primarily with the written form of the documents.

THE REDACTION OF OLDER MATERIALS

Although the terms "redaction history" and "redaction criticism" have a special meaning in New Testament studies at the present time, they also refer to certain analogous efforts which are present in the study of the Old Testament. In the latter, the concern with the work of redaction is viewed as part of the history of tradition as a whole, representing the last stages in which a final stamp is put upon the formation of a work. Thus, rather than representing any separate kind of approach, the interest in the work of the redactors of certain parts of the Old Testament is encompassed by traditio-historical method.

At the same time, the word "redactor" has experienced a transformation in meaning as it is presently used. In the earlier usage of this term in documentary criticism, the word was employed to designate some supposedly unknown person or persons who were essentially collectors of older sources or traditions, and who devoted themselves to interweaving these sources into a complex literary tapestry. Far from being viewed as creative people, the redactors were thought of as rather prosaic men who contributed little to the basic content and intention of the documents. All this has changed, however, with more recent study of the literature by tradition and redaction critics. For the latter, the redactors are seen as persons responsible for making their own contribution to the presentation of the tradition. In addition, since it is essentially from their hand that we have the final edition of the literature of the Old Testament, it is their viewpoint and conception of the structure and meaning of the Old Testament traditions which is most immediately evident in the literature itself.

Apart from the Scandinavian tradition historians, whose emphasis on oral tradition has led them in different directions, many tradition historians make use of the older insights gained from source criticism as an element in their own work. Thus they accept the conclusions of source critcism regarding the final redactoral work done by such anonymous people as the Yahwist or the Deuteronomist(s). In the case of each of these, many older traditions lie behind their final work. But the redactors represent some of the last to lay their hands on this ı ,aterial before it achieved canonical form.

Martin Noth's well-known work on the Deuteronomic History pays attention to features which can be said to belong to a redaction history of that work.[36] Like Engnell, Noth contended that the books of Joshua through Kings do not represent the continuation of certain of the sources isolated by documentary criticism in the Tetrateuch. Rather, these books are made up of an amalgam of traditions, to which Noth also gave the name Deuteronomic History. As they now lie before us, they are held together by the theological viewpoint of the Deuteronomic historian. Writing at the time of the exile of Jehoiachin ιο Babylon, the Deuteronomist attempted to present Israel's history from the time of Moses to the calamity of the exile as a history in which God's faithfulness to the promise given to the patriarchs continues, even though Israel is often wayward in her deeds.

From a traditio-historical perspective, what is important in the Deuteronomist's history is the process by which older blocks of tradition have come to be included in this work. According to Noth, the core of the work is the section in Deuteronomy 4:44–30:20, a clearly older deposit which served as the matrix for the construction of the work. But, in addition to this, there are complexes of stories and legends, as well as official annals from the archives of the state, which have been incorporated as well. There is the poetic Song of Moses in Deuteronomy 32, the so-called etiological stories and hero legends in Joshua 1–11, the Samson story from Judges 13–16, or the ark narrative from 1 Samuel 4:1b–7:1, to cite only several

36. Martin Noth, *Überlieferungsgeschichtliche Studien*, 2d ed. (Tübingen: Max Niemeyer Verlag, 1957).

of the traditions. All of this material, originating in both north and south, is introduced into a framework supplied by the Deuteronomic historian himself. And Noth takes great pains in his analysis to identify those sections (*Rahmenstücke*) by which the historian has tied his work together. However, it is just by attention to these latter that the theological viewpoint with which the work is constructed can be most readily seen.

This chapter, then, has been concerned with the problems of transmission encountered by Old Testament tradition historians. Two points can be made in summing up this discussion. In the first place, it should be evident that attention to the transmission problems is of great value for clarifying the message of the Old Testament texts. Such study shows that the Old Testament texts have experienced development over long periods of time. Different generations have taken them up, either in oral or written form, and transposed them into fresh settings and understandings. The effort to trace this process belongs to the study of transmission, and by examining the texts in this fashion, it is frequently possible to recover meanings buried deeply within them.

A second point can also be suggested. The study of the transmission of the texts demonstrates the movement of the Old Testament traditions toward the canonical form which they eventually acquire. The formation of the canon of Old Testament literature is not an arbitrary process connected with a particular historical period. It is inherent in the transmission of the Old Testament literature from early times. In the case of certain types of literature, like legal collections, the form may even have been fixed rather early, while in the case of other types, such as poetry and song, considerable modification may have occurred in the course of their transmission. In any event, we can observe very early a certain care in passing on the Old Testament traditions. Much later, under the pressures of the postexilic age, the community would gather together the various groups of literature and begin to regard them as normative writings. Thus the formation of the canon is really the last stage in the history of the transmission of the Old Testament literature.

II

The Formation of
Old Testament Traditions

The transmission problems discussed in the previous chapter are not the only matters with which tradition history is concerned. Important as they are, they are accompanied by other areas of investigation equally as significant. Further examination of the problem of transmission leads on to study of the processes involved in the formation of the Old Testament literature. Therefore, the problem of composition and transmission cannot be taken in isolation. To understand the way the literature of the Old Testament came into being, it is also necessary to get at the forces which were at work on the many different kinds of people who produced and transmitted this literature.

TRADITION AND TRADITIONISTS

As tradition historians attempt to explore the forces and influences behind the formation of the Old Testament, their study takes them in at least four important directions. First, such investigation inquires about the community or group responsible for the shaping and transmission of a particular tradition. This does not rule out the fact that specific individuals contributed to the formation of Old Testament literature. Certainly that would be the case with many types of literature such as the prophetic books. However, this kind of study assumes that even creative individuals would be more apt to reflect the themes and memories important for the group to which they belonged. And they would also tend to employ a certain kind of language and formulaic speech at home among their special group. The relation of a segment of tradition to the beliefs and functions of particular circles serves, therefore, to open up one important way at getting at its inner meaning and significance.

Several examples will illustrate this connection of particular groups with tradition. Among the ancient Israelites an important group was the priestly circle. The priests were long associated with the various sanctuaries, and naturally assumed the role of caretakers of old and sacred traditions and practices. Thus we find deposits of tradition about sacrifices and offerings, rubrics for cultic practices, and details of priestly equipment and activity, which have been handed on by groups interested in such things. For instance, the narrative sections of the Pentateuch are frequently interrupted by blocks of material deriving from these circles (Exod. 35–40, Num. 1:1–10:10). In addition, certain historical traditions, embracing the memory of past events which formed Israel, were also guarded and passed on by traditionists of the priestly class. Documentary critics had already noticed these materials in its P source. The contributions of this group did not cease even as late as the postexilic period, for during this time the Books of Chronicles provide evidence of a continuing influence at the hands of the successors of this group.

Some of the documentary critics, following Wellhausen, have dated the institution of priesthood in Israel to the late period of the postexilic age. They proposed that the priestly stratum of the Old Testament must represent the last stages of the development of Israelite religion.[1] But just here can be seen one of the important advances of more recent study. Traditio-historical study, along with archaeology and the comparative study of ancient Near Eastern literature and religion, has demonstrated the antiquity of both the priestly circles and parts of the priestly tradition of the Old Testament.[2] We must recognize, therefore, the influence that came from this group in mediating memories and traditions from early times on-

1. For a rather recent treatment see Robert H. Pfeiffer, *Introduction to the Old Testament* (New York: Harper & Bros., 1948), pp. 188–209.
2. William F. Albright, *From the Stone Age to Christianity*, 2d ed. (Garden City: Doubleday Anchor Books, 1957), pp. 252–54.

ward. Since their interests concentrated on the activity of the cultic centers, it is not surprising that we find the richness of the worship of ancient Israel preserved in their traditions.

A further example of an influential group can be found in the case of the Book of Deuteronomy. It is in connection with this book that von Rad has made one of his important contributions to Old Testament study.[3] By means of form critical and traditio-historical analysis, he showed how the Book of Deuteronomy makes use of old sacral and legal traditions, which are presented, however, in a preaching or homiletic style. Taking his cue from a statement in Nehemiah 8:7-8, von Rad suggested that the people responsible for this characteristic style of exhortation and instruction may have been preachers whose background was among Levitical circles.[4] This proposal, that a particular group stood behind the formation of Deuteronomy, is of fundamental importance, therefore, for von Rad's well-known interpretation of this book.[5]

Further examples can be found of still other groups involved in the shaping of certain Old Testament traditions. There is the role that wise men played in the creation and transmission of Israel's didactic and wisdom literature. There are the groups whose work resulted in what we know as the prophetic collections. Tradition history is interested in examining the history and character of these circles just because such data is valuable for understanding the meaning of the traditions themselves. By means of such study, we are often able to penetrate to the mind and ideology of these groups, and thus to understand better their intentions in transmitting certain traditions.

THE LOCALIZATION OF TRADITION

A second area which tradition history sees as important is the particular geographical location or locations with which a tradition was associated. Although this is closely related to the previous concern, the study of the localization of a tradition is

3. Gerhard von Rad, *Studies in Deuteronomy*, Studies in Biblical Theology, no. 9 (London: SCM Press, 1953).
4. Ibid., see especially chapter 1.
5. Von Rad's views, however, have been challenged recently by E. W. Nicholson, *Deuteronomy and Tradition* (Philadelphia: Fortress Press, 1967), pp. 83–87.

an important area of investigation in itself, and it is profitable to emphasize its importance separately. If a tradition can be isolated as being connected with a particular locale, then a thorough study of that site or area, along with the circles most intimately associated with it, can often produce significant new dimensions for its interpretation.

By means of traditio-historical study, it can sometimes be determined that a tradition originated in a specific area or at a particular site. One segment of the Jacob traditions discussed in the following chapter, for example, is related to the site of Bethel. And since the Jacob traditions associated with Bethel all have to do with intimate oracles received by the patriarch, and the latter's response in the form of cultic actions, they are important for understanding the role that Bethel, as a cultic site, played in the shaping and transmission of the Jacob tradition.

The significance of Shechem as a site important for the formation of Old Testament tradition has become apparent in recent study of covenant and treaty patterns in the ancient Near East. Form critical and comparative studies of such patterns have resulted in some far-reaching changes in our understanding of the Old Testament. By demonstrating the parallels between the covenant form of the Old Testament and surviving treaties between overlords and vassals from the surrounding regions, the antiquity of the covenant traditions has been demonstrated.[6] These studies have brought a necessary correction to earlier views, such as those of Wellhausen, that the covenant was a late form. As a corollary to this, the premonarchical period of old Israel, comprising the period of the settlement and the early tribal confederation during the twelfth and eleventh centuries B.C., is now generally seen as a formative period for the religion of the Old Testament. Some of the covenant traditions in the D history must have originated in and around Shechem (Deut. 27; Josh. 24; Judg. 9). The particular character of the Shechemite cultus is still very much debated, but there is growing consensus that this site,

6. For a lucid discussion of this area of study, see Delbert Hillers, *Covenant: The History of a Biblical Idea* (Baltimore: Johns Hopkins Press, 1969).

and its sanctuary, served as the focus for some of the most influential of old Israel's tradition and belief. Archaeological work on the mound at Tell Balâṭah has uncovered a series of sanctuaries which extend down to the period of the Israelite settlement, and this offers further testimony to the importance of ancient Shechem.[7]

Yet another site with which certain deposits of tradition are associated is that of Jerusalem. The increasing importance of this city from the Davidic-Solomonic age on is reflected in various places in the Old Testament. Since this site had a significant Canaanite history prior to its incorporation into the Davidic Empire, traditio-historical investigation has been interested in examining how the transition was made to Israelite belief, and what, if anything, might have been carried over from Canaanite antecedents in the traditions associated with Jerusalem. Both the motif of Mount Zion and the theology associated with the Solomonic temple originated here.

The Norwegian scholar, Sigmund Mowinckel, has carefully investigated the significance of Jerusalem as a center for Old Testament tradition.[8] Starting with the psalms, but using also other materials about Jerusalem, Mowinckel developed an interpretation of many parts of the Old Testament, in which the cultic significance of Jerusalem was held to play a central role. In his work, therefore, we have a special concentration on the history of cultic worship related to the concerns of tradition history.

Mowinckel's investigation suggests the following conclusions: First, the kingship and the Solomonic temple, both centered in Jerusalem, combined to bring wholly new motifs into Israelite faith and worship. Second, both kingship and temple played significant roles in an Israelite cultic celebration of the New Year festival, which enacted Yahweh's continued lordship over chaos. Third, the theme of the lordship of Yahweh as creator was consequently fundamental for this cultic tradition of Jerusalem, and it served also as the background for the

7. G. Ernest Wright, *Shechem: The Biography of a Biblical City* (London: G. Duckworth, 1965), pp. 80–122.
8. Sigmund Mowinckel, *The Psalms in Israel's Worship*, trans. D. R. Ap-Thomas, 2 vols. (New York: Abingdon Press, 1962).

eschatological portraits which begin to appear in some of the prophets. Finally, this whole tradition points to certain parallels between Israel and Mesopotamia, such as the New Year festival itself, although there are distinctive characteristics in the Israelite cult.

The great importance of Mowinckel's work, along with that of other scholars who have contributed to this same area of study, is that it has illuminated the role of Jerusalem in the formation of parts of the Old Testament tradition. While others have concentrated their attention on a northern site like Shechem, Mowinckel's work has shed greater light on the core of tradition associated with the south. Although important from the age of David onward, Jerusalem assumes an even more central role for the final shape of the Old Testament traditions during the later part of the Old Testament period. In fact, one of the more complicated processes to be seen in the history of the Old Testament literature occurs when, after the northern Israelite calamity in 722/1 B.C., the northern traditions are preserved and reworked into those of the surviving Judean kingdom, with its center in Jerusalem. Traditio-historical investigation shows that this has been the case with such varied works as the Deuteronomic History and some of the earlier north Israelite prophetic books, as well as the Book of Psalms.

These last observations suggest that not only specific sites, but also larger regions, may be significant for determining the locus of particular traditions.[9] Since the divisions which existed from an early time between the northern and southern tribal groups never were overcome, even in the age of David, it was inevitable that certain themes were preserved by the northern Israelites as over against others which were peculiar to their southern kinsmen. Thus, much of Old Testament study based on the history of tradition is inclined to speak of traditions preserved in these broad regional areas as northern Israelite, or southern Judean, or Jerusalemite, traditions. It now seems

9. Along with the differences of opinion about whether the Levites have preserved and transmitted the traditions of Deuteronomy, note the disagreement between von Rad and Nicholson on the question of a northern or southern provenance for Deuteronomy (cf. the references in notes 3 and 5).

clear that the traditions of the exodus from Egypt and of the Mosaic covenant were carried on predominantly by north Israelite circles, while those of the kingship and the inviolability of Mount Zion originated and were preserved in the south. With such fundamental localization of tradition in mind, it is helpful to discern how the variety of Old Testament literature finds itself related to this or that tradition. Thus in the Psalter, for example, there are psalms which suggest their northern Israelite provenance by means of the themes upon which they build (e.g., Pss. 29, 42). Similarly, the prophetic books are characterized often by the similarity of their language to that of one or the other traditions.

The importance of the localization of a tradition, or even a book, can thus be seen to have great importance for the meaning of the literature under question. By inquiring into the experiences and memories which were of special importance at a site or in a region, it is possible to achieve new perspectives upon the material. This holds even for very late literature such as the traditions collected in the Book of Daniel. The problems of the localization of this apocalyptic material, different though they may be from other types of Old Testament literature, must be dealt with in order to gain an overall perspective for interpreting this late work.

SOCIAL, POLITICAL, AND RELIGIOUS DYNAMICS IN TRADITION

If traditio-historical study is interested in determining with what circles and with what location a piece of literature is associated, it is also concerned with certain dynamics that are present in the origin and reformulation of a tradition. These include sociological, political, or cultic influences which might have been operative in the production of a particular literature. Fundamentally this is what the form critic means by the phrase "setting in life." The historian of tradition finds his attention drawn very closely to certain features in the life of the circles who produced and transmitted a tradition, and which may have been influential in their creation and development of other traditions. This approach to the Old Testament material demands, therefore, an intimate acquaintance with the sociology of ancient Israel and the history of her political and cultic institutions, as well as a knowledge of the history of events themselves.

In discussing Mowinckel's contributions, the institutional role that cult sometimes played in relation to the literary remains of the Old Testament was noted. There is compelling evidence that certain cultic settings served as some sort of institutional framework for different kinds of literature in the Old Testament. It is instructive to note how von Rad combines study of a number of institutional backgrounds, at different points, in presenting his interpretation of the Book of Deuteronomy. On the one hand, von Rad's proposal is that the Book of Deuteronomy is modeled on an ancient covenant form. In studying this form, von Rad observed that "the remarkable way in which parenesis, laws, binding by covenant, blessing and cursing follow upon one another"[10] points to the basic formulations of a great cultic ceremony. Von Rad concluded that the Book of Deuteronomy, therefore, must have had its ultimate roots in an annal feast of covenant renewal celebrated at Shechem.[11]

But, this original cultic milieu, in which much of Deuteronomy was given its shape, does not account for all aspects of the book, or the role that it assumed later during the reign of Josiah. Here some important discussion of political institutions and revivalist tendencies at the time of Josiah enters the picture.[12] Von Rad reflected on the central role that the old institution of holy war plays in the ideology of the book, and this led him to inquire further as to what sociological and political conditions could best explain the important role this old institution plays in this book. The solution he proposed was that, after 701 B.C., with the surrender of the Israelite mercenary troops to the Assyrians, the old-style militia from the days of the tribal federation was revived. This earlier form of the military received strong support from the landed gentry, von Rad's interpretation of the "people of the land" (*'am hā'āretz*) mentioned prominently during the reign of Josiah. Such conditions explain the place that older traditions, such as those of

10. Von Rad, *Studies in Deuteronomy*, p. 14.
11. Ibid., pp. 40–41.
12. Ibid., pp. 60–69.

the Sinai covenant, have in the book. They also indicate how an older institution, like that of holy war, could find new roots in the unsettled social and political situation developing during the seventh century. Similar forces continued at work into the reign of Josiah, and these von Rad sees as influential in the formation of the Book of Deuteronomy.

This example shows, therefore, how a diversity of social, political, and cultic elements can be pursued in tracing the development of tradition in certain books of the Old Testament. Parallel efforts could be cited for the study of the Pentateuchal traditions and the prophetic books, and they have also been taken up more recently in regard to the wisdom literature.

THEMES AND MOTIFS IN TRADITION

Perhaps no aspect of traditio-historical research is so important, especially for the content and message of the Old Testament, as its study of various themes of the Old Testament. Such investigation involves an intricate search for the way particular themes came to be formulated, and the role they continued to play as they were brought into different contexts in the course of time. Two scholars who have contributed to such thematic research in the study of Old Testament tradition are Gerhard von Rad and Martin Noth. Although aspects of their work have already been mentioned, it is interesting to observe how they handle this special problem.

Von Rad's contribution was presented in a monograph on the problem of the Hexateuch which appeared in 1938.[13] Beginning with the assumption that the basic form of the Hexateuch reflected an originally cultic background, von Rad discussed three sections, Deuteronomy 26:5b–9, Deuteronomy 6:20–24, and Joshua 24:2b–13, as containing the remnants of what he called "a small historical credo."[14] In each of these

13. Gerhard von Rad, "Das Formgeschichtliche Problem des Hexateuchs," in *Gesammelte Studien zum Alten Testament*, Theologische Bücherei, no. 8 (München: Christian Kaiser Verlag, 1961), pp. 9–86. This article has now been translated into English under the title "The Form-Critical Problem of the Hexateuch," in Gerhard von Rad, *The Problem of the Hexateuch and Other Essays*, trans. E. W. T. Dicken (New York: McGraw-Hill, 1966), pp. 1–78.
14. Ibid., pp. 3–8.

confessions the basic theme is the occupation of the land, while the exodus and wilderness themes are also incorporated. In other words, these confessions point to early cultic celebrations of the key themes about the saving deeds of Yahweh, which are the fundamental formulae for expressing the canonical faith.

It was in the context of this discussion that von Rad stated his controversial interpretation of the Sinai tradition. Since none of the confessions alludes to the Sinai theme, von Rad proposed that the latter must originally have been independent of the exodus and land allocation themes.[15] Von Rad argued that it was only with the Yahwist historian that the Sinai complex was introduced into the basic confessional framework, just as it was the Yahwist who expanded the history backwards to include the patriarchal traditions, and who for the first time incorporated a "primeval history." But even this effort of the Yahwist did not achieve common acceptance, and it was only in later prayers, such as Psalm 106 and Nehemiah 9, that the Sinai theme finally came to be assumed as an element in the canonical scheme. While the exodus and land allocation themes celebrated the mighty deeds of Yahweh, the Sinai theme built on the notions of divine theophany and covenant. Concerning the sites with which these traditions were connected, von Rad concluded that the Sinai theme must have been associated with Shechem and specifically with the Feast of Tabernacles as a "covenant renewal feast," while the exodus and land acquisition themes were preserved at Gilgal, and in relation to the Feast of Weeks.[16]

Martin Noth also paid careful attention to themes in his works, and his well-known study on the Pentateuch provides an illustration.[17] Noth accepted von Rad's view of the Pentateuch as the expansion of an early cultic confessional form, and proceeded to work further in his own study of the formation of these traditions. He viewed the growth of the first five books

15. Ibid., pp. 13–20. For a critique of this position see G. Ernest Wright, *The Old Testament and Theology* (New York: Harper & Row, 1969), pp. 61–66.
16. Von Rad, "The Form-Critical Problem of the Hexateuch," pp. 33–48.
17. Martin Noth, *Überlieferungsgeschichte des Pentateuch* (Stuttgart: W. Kohlhammer Verlag, 1948).

of the Old Testament around the development of five basic themes: (1) the deliverance from Egypt, (2) the settlement in the land, (3) the promise to the patriarchs, (4) the leadership in the wilderness, and (5) the revelation at Sinai.

According to Noth, each of these themes has its own traditio-historical problems. The exodus theme seems to have been preserved by several clans who later joined with tribal groups settling in the land, and it was this theme which subsequently served to catalyze the various confederating groups. The settlement in the land theme originally had nothing to do with the exodus complex, but became linked to the former as the diverse traditions were consolidated. The theme of the promise to the patriarchs has a more complicated history. Each of the clans appears to have possessed some tradition of its patriarch, and in the Pentateuch these have been worked together into a prehistory of Israel. The wilderness theme represented originally a tradition of southern clans until it was brought into relation with the other themes. And finally, regarding the Sinai tradition, Noth accepted the view of von Rad that this also was originally an independent tradition, only secondarily connected to the exodus and land acquisition themes.[18]

Each theme, therefore, is viewed as having its own history before it became part of the larger literary complex of the Pentateuch. In the course of time, as they are brought into relation with each other, these themes become key elements in the framework of the Pentateuch, and the great amount of material in the Pentateuch is brought together around them. Noth's study, then, is devoted to a close examination of the development of this variegated material as it is brought into conjunction with these fundamental themes.

TRADITION HISTORY AND THE PROBLEM OF
HISTORICAL CREDIBILITY

The discussion up to this point makes it apparent that tradition history studies the Old Testament material from a particular perspective. According to its understanding, history

18. Ibid., pp. 63–64.

encompasses more than the presentation of simple facts. Rather, historical memory in the Old Testament is viewed as being accompanied by interpretations by which the community sought the meaning of those recollections. This concentration on the depth of events and experiences is what made the historian of the Old Testament, in the words of Edmund Jacob, "the brother of the poet."[19]

Such an emphasis on creative elements leads, however, to some basic questions concerning the nature of the Old Testament traditions. Simply put, the issue is: To what degree are these traditions reliable accounts of that which they relate? The fact that the very word tradition itself sometimes carries the meaning of something fabricated highlights the difficulties inherent in this particular kind of question.

In responding to this problem, the approach of the historian may range from one accompanied by a certain skepticism, on the one hand, to one which grants the biblical tradition as much dependability as possible, on the other. These are the two poles, and in making historical judgments about the documents, different interpreters can be found at any number of places in between. It may even happen that in the cases of some texts the interpreter will lean toward one appraisal, while the weight of the evidence will convince him differently in regard to others.

An example which has almost become classic by now is the manner in which two important historians have assessed the patriarchal traditions of the Old Testament. On the one hand, the German scholar, Martin Noth, gave a large place to the role of creativity in the formation of these traditions. This was particularly apparent in his use of the principle of etiology. In general his approach assumed that the documents about the patriarchs cannot be used as history in our modern sense.[20] On the other hand, William F. Albright, while also allowing for the fact that these stories are obviously not history in the same sense as modern historical writing, has held that the

19. Edmund Jacob, *La Tradition historique en Israël*, Études théologiques et religieuses (Montpellier: Faculté de Théologie Protestante, 1946), p. 8.
20. Martin Noth, *The History of Israel*, trans. P. R. Ackroyd, 2d ed. (New York: Harper & Bros., 1960), pp. 121–27.

archaeological evidence provides more substantial support for the broad historicity of the patriarchal period as a whole. His approach has led him to the historical judgment that the biblical tradition has transmitted a collection of reasonably reliable recollections of the patriarchal history. As Albright has viewed them, the patriarchal narratives are prose adaptations of older versified oral tradition which probably had its rootage in the Middle Bronze Age. He has found support for this interpretation in the increasing amount of archaeological and textual data from sites like Mari and Ugarit. Albright's contention is that this material makes it impossible to hold any longer that the patriarchal traditions are basically late creations, as much scholarship after Wellhausen has continued to do.[21]

This example shows how two historians who recognize the role of tradition in the ancient Near East arrive at different estimations of these traditions. The approach of Albright and others has been to grant the basic authenticity of the texts and traditions until they are shown to be otherwise by historical and archaeological study. This procedure in biblical studies is parallel in some ways to the reassessment in Homeric studies which has been necessitated by recent historical and archaeological study of Troy and the Trojan War.[22] Other scholars, as has been seen, have seemed to operate with a greater degree of skepticism in studying the Old Testament materials. However, even if the results of this latter approach have often been negative and have had to be revised or abandoned in the light of comparative study, they have often served to prod evaluations which have been too facile. And not a few times they have brought forth significant insights into the nature and development of the faith of the Old Testament.

These two approaches, therefore, have frequently served to complement each other, even in their tension with each other,

---

21. William F. Albright, *History, Archaeology and Christian Humanism* (New York: McGraw-Hill, 1964), pp. 28–30. For a similar positive assessment see Roland de Vaux, "Les Patriarches hébreux et l'Histoire," in *Bible et Orient* (Paris: Les Éditions du Cerf, 1968), pp. 175–85.
22. See the remarks of de Vaux in *The Bible in Modern Scholarship*, ed. J. Philip Hyatt (Nashville: Abingdon Press, 1965), p. 29, n. 30.

and the mainstream of Old Testament scholarship has profited from them both. Thus, at this stage of Old Testament study the most promising procedure seems to be for both approaches to continue to pursue their own methodologies to the best of their abilities. This will permit the assessment of fundamental differences and tensions between them, as well as the possibility of achieving a synthesis at certain points. In this way both have much to contribute to the theological meaning of the Old Testament.

III

Tradition History
and Hebrew Narrative

It is in the study of actual texts that a method must prove its validity. In this and the following chapter, therefore, we have selected two biblical sections for treatment, one a narrative section from the Pentateuch, the other a prophetic book. These two examples, representing quite diverse types of literature in the Old Testament, should serve to bring into clearer focus the range of problems encountered in traditio-historical study of Old Testament texts.

THE JACOB CYCLE

Even a cursory reading of the narratives of Genesis dealing with Jacob suffices to show that the section is comprised of various episodes which have been brought together to form a whole. When we study this section closely, however, we are moved to ask about the background of these narratives. How did they take shape, and how were the different units of tradition formed and transmitted? Does the story of Jacob contain originally independent episodes which were brought together in the course of the amalgamation of these traditions in ancient Israel? If they were originally independent, what was their earlier meaning and significance? And how does the meaning change as a tradition is incorporated into a larger complex and ultimately into a later work? What about the geographical and regional background of some of the episodes, and how are these connected with each other? Is it possible to identify particular groups of individuals from whose hands these traditions of Jacob have derived? All of these questions, suggested by the general discussion above, become pertinent when this interesting narrative is examined more closely.

Looked at as a whole, the Jacob cycle contains several groupings of material. First, there are accounts dealing with the rivalry between Jacob and Esau, found in Genesis 25:19–34, 27:1–45, 32:3–21, and 33:1–17. Second, Jacob is sent off to the original Aramaean homeland of his parents in upper Mesopotamia, and here the Jacob-Laban episodes are located, as related in Genesis 27:46–28:9, and 29:1–32:2. It is also with this cycle of material that the birth of Jacob's sons is connected (Gen. 29:31–30:24), which has further links to the Joseph narrative of Genesis and, indeed, the remainder of the Pentateuch. Finally, a last and significant complex of material has to do with divine theophanies which take place at several sites of cultic importance. One such theophany occurs at Bethel in Genesis 28:10–22, which is taken up again in 35:1–15. A second occurs in relation to the Trans-Jordan site of Penuel in Genesis 32:22–32, and a third at Shechem in 33:18–20.

What becomes apparent in examining these basic complexes of material in the Jacob cycle is that they have passed through various stages in an intricate process leading to the form in which we now have them. If one looks, for example, at the transition from the episode about Jacob's deceit in regard to the paternal blessing to that of his flight to Laban, there are indications that these two cycles may not have been originally related. That is suggested in the Jacob-Laban cycle itself, which has its own set of motifs and themes, and is not integrally linked to the flight theme of the Jacob-Esau cycle. A connection between the two cycles is made only with the transition section in Genesis 27:43–45, while the linkage is very loose following Jacob's later flight from Laban back into Esau territory (Gen. 32:3–4). This is underscored further by the presence of a second tradition in Genesis 27:46–28:5, in which Jacob is encouraged by his parents to go to Aram, not in order to flee from the wrath of Esau but rather to obtain a wife from his own ancestral line. That Esau fails to do so, but rather carries out the odious act of marrying a Hittite wife (Gen. 28:6–9), represents an extension of the theme of this tradition.

Further, the theophanies also betray a certain independence, although the traditionists have incorporated them at critical points in the narrative. The theophany at Bethel (Gen. 28:10–22) deals with the particular sanctity of this site, to which the themes of promise of land and offspring are added. The assurance of divine protection at Bethel makes a rather easy link to the flight from Esau motif, although the latter is nowhere explicit in the Bethel theophany tradition. Also in the case of the Penuel encounter in Genesis 32:22–32, there is every indication that this is a unit in itself, and there is nothing in the episode which would suggest whether the divine strength and assurance received in these encounters is directed toward the flight from Laban or the impending encounter with Esau. However, the traditionists have in both cases placed these crucial theophanies at those points where flight and jeopardy are at their most extreme. In the case of the Bethel episode it is in the haste with which Jacob must flee the anger of his brother, while in the case of the encounter at Penuel it is at that critical juncture where the patriarch is wholly dependent upon divine protection as he leaves one threatening situation and moves into another.

The traditio-historical problems which arise, then, must take account of the way these episodes have been incorporated into larger complexes to produce a more unified narrative. Source criticism has contributed an intricate kind of analysis of these chapters. According to the source critics, the chapters are predominantly made up of the fusion of Yahwist and Elohist elements, with the former being somewhat larger in the bulk of material than the latter. P is present in Genesis 25:19–20, 26b; 27:46–28:9; 31:18a&b; 33:18a; 35:6, 9–13a, 15. Many contemporary scholars still follow the lines of the source analysis of this section, represented best of all, perhaps, in Martin Noth's intricate work on the Pentateuch cited above. At the same time, there is a growing recognition of older traditional material in these narratives, as is also indicated in Noth's work. For those who follow the lines of tradition history laid out by Engnell, the efforts to pursue actual source material here are thought to be misleading. Yet, the grounds for totally abandoning such analysis remain to be justified.

and the argument on this crucial issue is by no means over. In this section, therefore, we shall follow the more common procedure of calling attention to source critical divisions at certain points. At the same time, our intent will be to set the Jacob narrative into the framework of the traditio-historical questions.

If the interesting and diverse complexes of material in the Jacob narrative suggest an intricate process in the development of this material, there are also other factors which are of significance. There is the matter of the localization of this narrative material. It is noteworthy that the materials of the Jacob cycle are related to three or four geographical areas. First, there is the importance of the Bethel-Shechem region, with which a cluster of the material is associated. Again, at least some of the material refers to the region of Edom, such as the Esau story and its allusions to the territory of Seir. The area east of the Jordan, specifically the land of Gilead, is related to part of the narrative, including the Mahanaim and Penuel episodes, as well as the confrontation between Jacob and Laban (Gen. 31:25). And finally, the importance of the region of upper Mesopotamia, the homeland of Laban, has already been noted.

Our procedure now will be to examine the several complexes in some detail, dealing with their own inner problems and the insights that a traditio-historical approach brings to these. This will be followed by a discussion of the problem of the meaning of the narrative as a whole.

JACOB AND ESAU

The specific material dealing with the theme of Jacob and Esau is found in the following places. Genesis 25:19–26 reports the circumstances surrounding the birth of the twins who are destined to be in rivalry with one another. The section in 25:27–34 is a self-contained unit concerning the transference of the birthright. In 27:1–45 a further unit portrays the ruse by which Jacob manages to obtain the special paternal blessing. The anger of Esau in consequence of this deceit provides the reason and background for the flight of Jacob to the east.

The next point at which specifically Jacob-Esau material is met is found upon the return of Jacob from the region of Laban. In 32:3–21 Jacob prepares for the encounter with Esau. This is followed up in 33:1–16 with the description of an unexpected filial encounter between the rival parties, resulting in a relation of mutual accord.

If we look at these units separately—an essential preliminary work in attempting to find the intent in the overlay and development of tradition—it is sometimes possible to discern a number of levels of meaning in them. The section in 25:19–26 serves as an introduction to the narrative as a whole, by providing the background of the birth of Jacob and Esau. After a brief and incomplete genealogical notice from P in 25:19–20, the notice of Isaac's prayer regarding the barren womb of Rebekah is given a divine answer in 25:21. The account then begins to play on descriptions and words which are a marked characteristic of this narrative and certainly belong to developing meanings seen in the tradition in the course of its transmission. The "struggle" of the children within the womb, the oracle about the two nations ($g\bar{o}yim$) divided from each other, the hairiness ($s\bar{e}^{c}\bar{a}r$) of Esau suggesting Seir and his redness ($'\bar{a}d\bar{o}m$) intimating Edom, all point to particular emphases achieved in the growth of this tradition. There is a distinct contrast between two ways of life represented by the hunter, Esau, and the shepherd, Jacob. In addition, the detail of the second taking hold of the heel ($^{c}\bar{a}q\bar{e}bh$) of the firstborn provides an explanation for the name Jacob itself, one which, however, does not represent the original meaning of this name.[1] Nevertheless, the purpose of this preliminary material is clear, in that it sets the stage for the further playing with the theme of rivalry.

In 25:27–34, there follows the first of two independent units drawing out the theme of rivalry, and Jacob's crafty dealings in obtaining superiority over his brother. For these two episodes it is best to use the technical form critical term, saga, and a word of explanation about that term is in order here.

---

1. The original name may have been $Y^{c}qb$-$'l$, "May God protect." See E. A. Speiser, *Genesis*, The Anchor Bible, vol. 1 (Garden City: Doubleday & Co., 1964), p. 197.

As we saw above, it was Hermann Gunkel who gave the clearest description of the role of saga in the Book of Genesis.[2] In his discussion of this form of presentation, Gunkel attempted to show how ancient folk literature is often less interested in presenting the history of social and political institutions than it is in mediating the memory of personal, family, or tribal experiences. Technically, therefore, saga is to be differentiated from history by means of its attachment to these latter,· the folk and tribal traditions. Gunkel does not mean to suggest that such traditions in saga form are unreliable or without historical worth. Rather, his effort is to clarify this particular form as a literary type in the Book of Genesis.

Gunkel's study makes several other points which are important for our understanding of these Jacob traditions. Since saga concentrates on matters of the family or tribe, what it transmits and how it transmits it are of special interest to groups living in the localities where the tradition is situated. At the same time, the imagination of saga is lively, being interested in such devices as wordplay, which, as we have seen above, is probably related to the oral form in which much of this literature was earlier transmitted.

In any event, such a description of saga fits well the episodes found in 25:27–34 and 27:1–45. Each of these units stands by itself, having a self-contained action. The interest is not in far-reaching problems, but rather in the interactions of several members of a family. As the story unfolds step by step, the listener is confronted by a series of briefly indicated tensions and is challenged to respond with a variety of emotions. These factors all point to a development which must go back into a period of oral presentation of these episodes.

Yet, the two traditions here evidently had a relationship to each other in their development which can no longer be traced. This is apparent in the association of words which provide the basic motifs of the two episodes. In the one saga, it is the birthright ($b^ek\bar{o}r\bar{a}h$) which is at stake, while in the second it is the blessing ($b^er\bar{a}k\bar{a}h$) of the father. The manner

2. See Gunkel's discussion in *The Legends of Genesis: The Biblical Saga and History*, trans. W. H. Carruth (New York: Schocken Books, 1964), pp. 1–12.

in which Jacob gains both of these from his brother is portrayed differently in the two episodes, however. In the first, Jacob appears as a matter-of-fact, opportunist personality in the face of his dull-witted brother who is willing to sell off his inheritance for the needs of the moment. In the second, Jacob, along with his mother, becomes party to a plan in which Esau is unfortunately trapped. Both stories thus play, in quite different ways, the theme of how Jacob outwits his brother and takes over his rights.

That something more is intended in these stories than what appears on the surface is also evident in 25:27. Here it can be seen that the listeners will not be thinking merely of two individuals, but they will also hear the nuance of two different ways of life. This fact is doubtless of great importance in determining the meaning of these sagas at certain stages in their transmission. Jacob belongs to the shepherd life, and is characterized as "a quiet man" (*tām*). He thus represents a more sedentary type of life, while Esau is depicted as the hunter, "a man of the field" (*'ish sādheh*).

As these stories were carried along in the tradition, such broader nuances of meaning were developed and perpetuated. Thus the pottage which Jacob was making in 25:29–30 is found in the Hebrew as *'ādōm*, and this quickly suggested the identification of Esau with Edom. In the second of the two episodes the play again is made on the root *'āqabh*, meaning to "supplant," and allusion is made to the extortion of both the birthright and the blessing (Gen. 27:36). In the blessings which are preserved in these two sagas, in 27:27–29 and 27:39–40, the contrast between the two types of people is again sketched out. To Jacob is promised fertility of the land while Esau will live "away" from the produce of the land, and will rather find his livelihood by the sword.

These two stories, then, are followed by a transition section in 27:41–45, which links the theme of the rivalry between the brothers with the traditions of Jacob's sojourn in the east. The leading motif here becomes the hate harbored by Esau, which necessitates the flight of the successful brother. Following this there is the interlude of the stay at Bethel and the Jacob-Laban cycle, which will be discussed in the next section.

It is only with the completion of the Jacob-Laban cycle that the theme of Jacob and Esau is taken up again. Here there are two sections, the preparations made by Jacob for his renewed encounter with Esau in 32:3–21 and the meeting itself in 33:1–17. Standing at the end of the Jacob cycle as a whole, this story of an impending encounter, after long years of separation, is accompanied by considerable tension. The narrative begins with the episode of Jacob's messengers making an initial contact with Esau (32:3–6). The report that Esau is approaching with his own forces of four hundred men strikes fear into the heart of Jacob, who responds in two ways. On the one hand he divides his own possessions and company (32:6–8) and, on the other, he attempts to bring about a favorable meeting by sending presents ahead to his brother (32:13–21). Source division has recognized parallel J and E traditions in these two motifs.

The resultant meeting in 33:1–17 brings an unexpected ending to the Jacob and Esau cycle, as the latter is said to fall on Jacob's neck and to kiss him (33:4). No reasons are cited as to what prompted this change of heart on the part of Esau to offer such gracious treatment to his brother. As the whole narrative now stands, the time that Jacob spends in the service of Laban serves at least to lead up to this reconciliation, for it represents a long "cooling off" period, a time during which Jacob himself goes through certain trials and thus is subjected to a process of repentance and maturing. Nevertheless, the theme of possible further deceit and craftiness continues, even in the final section. That Jacob refuses Esau's invitation to go with him in 33:15–16 is probably meant to suggest that the former still has some suspicion. Were he to go with Esau, the latter might well turn the tables on him once more.

We possess in the Jacob-Esau cycle, then, a series of episodes, some of which may be of considerable age, being found earlier in verse form. Both J and E have preserved some of this material, and it might be assumed that other materials fell by the way. In the J and E narratives these stories have been woven into a larger whole, as part of the larger Jacob narrative. However, in looking at the Jacob-Esau units themselves, it is possible to discern a smaller complex of material comprised of stories and anecdotes around the theme of the rivalry of the brothers.

Two questions now pose themselves. How is the Jacob-Esau cycle to be interpreted? And what should be made of the geographical locations of these stories? Regarding the first, we have already noted the way these stories intimate the relations between two particular groups or types of people. In the tradition itself there is the suggestion, on the one hand, of the contrast between shepherds and hunters, and on the other, of the relations of the descendants of Jacob with those of Esau, the Edomites.

Martin Noth has discussed this problem and has proposed the interpretation that the contrast between the shepherd and hunter type is probably the older of the two meanings, and that the connection of the Jacob-Esau cycle with the relations between Judah and Edom is a later overlay in the tradition.[3] If this is so, then the original significance of this material must be connected with an area where such a rivalry between hunters and shepherds would be likely. Noth suggested that the region east of the Jordan is well suited for just such relationships, since here there is the wooded area of the Jabbok region which would provide just the setting for this contrast of interests and life-styles.[4] For this reason Noth proposed that the Jacob-Esau cycle has its provenance in the Trans-Jordan area, in the region of Gilead, and its connections with the area west of the Jordan are only made subsequently, when this material is incorporated as part of the larger Jacob narrative. Since the tribe of Ephraim possessed for some time a colonized region in this area east of the Jordan, it was Noth's suggestion that these episodes represent traditions of the Ephraimites east of the Jordan. At the same time, it is not difficult to see how they could be brought into convergence with the Jacob traditions preserved west of the Jordan by related Ephraimites in the hill country.

The most important factor which favors this interpretation of Noth's is the episode of the meeting of Jacob and Esau in

3. Noth, *Überlieferungsgeschichte des Pentateuch* (Stuttgart: W. Kohlhammer Verlag, 1948), pp. 104–5.
4. Ibid., p. 107.

the region of Mahanaim and Penuel, near the Jabbok river. Noth recalled that these sites are a great distance from Edom, and thus it hardly seems likely that an encounter between Edom and Israel would have taken place in the region where these episodes are located.[5] The Edomite-Israelite motif must accordingly represent a later layer imposed on this tradition. Nevertheless, Noth's interpretation does not need to be taken as final, and, in any event, the relation of the Jacob-Esau cycle to such ethnic interrelationships is necessary to pursue simply because of the important indications given in the tradition itself about this layer of meaning.

JACOB AND LABAN

As we have already noted, the Jacob-Laban cycle seems to stand on its own, without being dependent on the Jacob-Esau tradition. It is noteworthy that one point where a connection between the two is made is the transition in 27:41–45. Source critics assign this section to J, and it stresses the anger of Esau as being the cause of Jacob's flight to the east. As has also been noted, another tradition, commonly credited to P, is found in 27:46–28:9, which offers as the reason for the journey to Aram the desire on the part of Jacob's parents to keep the bloodline pure. In the P tradition no direct link is made with the stories of the Jacob-Esau cycle. This suggests that the Jacob-Laban material must be examined in itself before turning to the matter of how it is related to the larger narrative.

The Jacob-Laban cycle comprises a large complex of material found in 29:1–32:2. In contrast to the stories of Jacob and Esau, this section gives the impression of being a continuous narrative. The material divides into the reports of Jacob's appearance in the east (29:1–14), the two marriages of Jacob (29:15–30), the traditions of the sons of Jacob (29:31–30:24), the wealth of Jacob (30:25–43), the flight and pursuit narrative (31:1–42), and, finally, the treaty between Laban and Jacob (31:43–32:1).

The episode in 29:1–14 has all the marks of an old tradition. The scene is the meeting at the well, at which Jacob comes into contact with his kinsmen. This incident leads rather

5. Ibid., p. 105.

Laban. Up to this point Jacob's stay has been characterized by trial and disappointment. He has repeatedly been made to suffer by means of the clever devices of Laban. Now the narrative moves on to show how the fortunes of the patriarch are suddenly turned. Once again it might be noted that in saga such a motif, which stresses the way the main figure in the story advances from difficulty to achievement, would be a favorite one in the telling. Along with this, the intricate account of the rods, with all of its magical features, serves to bear up the motif of trial.

The flight and pursuit narrative in 31:1–42 sets forth two reasons as to why Jacob desires to return to his homeland. On the one hand, Laban's sons have charged that Jacob has deprived their father of much of his wealth (31:1–2), and, on the other, a divine command is given connecting the departure with the promise of the theophany at Bethel (31:3, 13). Thus Jacob gathers his family and flocks, and leaves without Laban's knowledge. The pursuit of the latter leads to an encounter which takes place in the region of Gilead, and this introduces one of the important units in the Jacob-Laban cycle.

That unit is the closing one of the cycle, and tells of a covenant between Laban and Jacob (31:43–32:1). The manner in which this act reflects widespread custom known from extrabiblical literature is striking.[9] It is also noteworthy that this tradition has carried on one of the Aramaic phrases in the Old Testament in the name Jegar-sahadutha (31:47), the stone heap attesting to the validity of the covenant. For Martin Noth this episode is the kernel of the Jacob-Laban cycle and it is in relation to it that he sees the filling out of the remainder of the material in the narrative.[10] Consequently he interprets the whole tradition of Jacob-Laban as once more suggesting relationships between Trans-Jordanian Israelites and their Aramaean neighbors immediately to the north. He does not think this needs to be as far north as the Euphrates region, and states his own preference for seeing it localized in the area of Gilead. However, this has the effect of eliminating the con-

9. Speiser, *Genesis*, p. 249.
10. Noth, *Überlieferungsgeschichte des Pentateuch*, pp. 100–111.

nection of the Jacob-Laban saga with the region around Haran, and it seems more likely that the latter location played an important role as geographical background for these stories.

This leads us now to ask about the importance of the Jacob-Laban cycle as a whole, and it can be stated simply that this cycle has a special significance. One reason for this is that scholarship is increasingly demonstrating the importance of the region of the upper Euphrates for the traditions about the ancestors of Israel. Such names as Haran, mentioned in the Abraham narrative, and Aram of the Jacob-Laban cycle, intend to place the original homeland of the patriarchs in this area. That an ongoing affiliation with this region is pointed to in the traditions of the patriarchs accords well with an increasing amount of archaeological data coming from this area. When the latter is put together with the biblical narratives, a picture emerges which suggests some sort of connection of the patriarchs with the Aramaeans and the region of Syria up to the Euphrates.

It is interesting, in this regard, to recall that one of the liturgical confessions, which tradition historians accept as old material, identifies Jacob as an Aramaean. It seems most likely that the words of this confession, "A wandering Aramean was my father . . ." (Deut. 26:5), refer to Jacob as the ancestor of Israel, whose roots were in the territory of Aram. The importance of the Jacob-Laban cycle, then, is just in this interesting connection that it has with the region called Paddan-aram in 31:18. Thus, once again we can see the importance of the element of localization in the formation, preservation, and meaning of tradition. At the same time, the treaty between Jacob and Laban may reflect larger political contacts between the eastern Israelites and their blood brothers, the Aramaeans. By the time of David such contacts, often acrimonious, are frequently found between Israel and her Aramaean neighbors to the northeast (2 Sam. 10:1–19).

We have stressed that the Jacob-Laban cycle stands on its own, with its own motifs being central to the unfolding of the narrative. At the same time, the cycle gains further meaning and significance through its eventual relationship to the narratives of Jacob-Esau. At whatever stage in the tradition these two cycles have come to be linked together, therefore, it is as a totality that their meaning is now found. In this larger relation the Jacob-Laban narrative comes to represent an interlude during which the threatened patriarch and his angry brother can live apart until, through trying circumstances such as those told only in the case of Jacob, they are brought together later in a new spirit of acceptance.

THE THEOPHANIES

Interspersed among the various episodes of the Jacob narrative is a series of divine encounters which are crucial in the career of the patriarch. In fact, as will be seen, it is these theophanies which provide a special depth to the experiences of the patriarch. Apart from them, the Jacob narrative tends to move with little sense of divine purpose operating in the earthy give and take of Jacob's dealings with both Esau and Laban. Unlike the two previous cycles which have been discussed, we are not dealing with a cycle in the case of the various theophanies which are found in the narrative. With the exception of the episodes about Bethel and Shechem, there seems to be no integral relation among the various traditions of theophanies. Thus, the two theophanies centered at the Trans-Jordan sites of Mahanaim and Penuel give no indication of having any direct relation to those at Bethel and Shechem, and appear to be independent traditions in their own right.

Recognition of this last factor has led tradition historians to propose that these theophany episodes in the Jacob narrative, as well as similar accounts in the other patriarchal traditions, reflect localized cult legends dealing with the particular sites to which these episodes are attached. In the case of Jacob, this involves the sites of Bethel and Shechem in the central hill country of Cis-Jordan, both of which are known elsewhere in the Old Testament to have important cultic significance. On the east side of the Jordan, similar theophanies occur at Mahanaim and Penuel, and it is possible that at the latter site some sort of sanctuary also existed. These theophanies, therefore, preserve the memory of the God of the patriarchs in a significant way. Even though the traditions have passed through much development as they lie before us, they contain recollections which put us into touch with various periods in the religion of the early Hebrews.

One significant question, especially important for the sites of Bethel and Shechem, is whether the theophany traditions have not been transferred to these sites at a later time when the tribal groups have settled in the hill country. Noth and others have argued that the divine appearances must have occurred elsewhere than at such sites in the arable land, since the patriarchs are described as a seminomadic people, related to the desert fringes. According to this interpretation, these traditions were then secondarily connected with the sites in the hill country, and these indeed had been old Canaanite sites prior to their adaptation into early Israelite tradition.[11] De Vaux, on the other hand, argues that all these sites stand along the line of demarcation between the arable land and the areas where sheepherding would have taken place, and thus they fit well the descriptions of groups in rather frequent movement found in these traditions. Consequently, de Vaux argues, there seems to be no compelling reason to deny the primary connection of these traditions with these sites.[12]

In discussing these theophanies, then, there are two main points with which we will concern ourselves in each case. First, there is the problem of the relation of the episode to the particular site with which it is associated. Second, it is necessary to see what function the theophany plays in the narrative where it is found.

The theophany in Genesis 28:10-22 deals with Jacob's visit to Bethel on his way to Haran. There are three main elements in the episode: the stone at which the patriarch sleeps and which he later sets up as a stele, the theophany itself along with the oracle, and the naming of the site. The pillar plays an important role in the story and suggests a certain background for it. Since such stelae are often associated with Canaanite worship, which is one of the reasons why orders are later given to tear them down (Deut. 12:3), this has been taken as one

11. Martin Noth, *The History of Israel*, trans. P. R. Ackroyd, 2d ed. (New York: Harper & Bros., 1960), pp. 121–23.
12. Roland de Vaux, *Ancient Israel* (New York: McGraw-Hill Paperbacks, 1965), p. 289.

indication of the fact that Bethel may have had a prehistory of Canaanite worship. If this is so, then the interpretation that this particular tradition has both taken over and supplanted originally Canaanite elements at this sanctuary may have some basis to it.

The description of the actual theophany is marked by several layers of meaning and intent, which is enough to suggest how important this Bethel tradition became as it was carried along. The account of the divine appearance itself contains a composite of two traditions, with the "heavenly ladder" (probably a ziggurat) representing E's description of the divine approach, while the J tradition contains an account in which God is said to be simply "next to him" (28:13). The oracle also indicates several levels of development and meaning. The latest links the promise to Jacob with that of Abraham in the twofold pledge of land and offspring (28:13–14), while what may be an earlier level connects the promise of divine protection with the patriarch's departure from the land until he can return once more (28:15). Finally, along with the act of anointing the pillar, the naming of the holy site takes place (28:19), supplying an etiology for the importance of the site in the worship of early Israel.

We have in this episode, then, an important tradition regarding the site of Bethel. In addition to this particular tradition, there is a further episode in 35:1–15, in which the patriarch is commanded to move on from Shechem to Bethel, and many of the same motifs as found in the earlier Bethel theophany are related once again. It is in connection with 35:10 that the name of Jacob is changed to Israel, a motif which, in turn, is found also in the East-Jordan episode of Penuel (Gen: 32:28). It is instructive to note how some of these motifs, like the one just mentioned, are found several times and are connected with different episodes. It is with such factors that the study of the history of tradition is concerned as it concentrates its attention on the problems of how such traditions developed and became attached to particular episodes and sites.

The episodes of Jacob at Bethel thus provide a foundation for the religious meaning of the site. For this reason some scholars refer to these stories as cult legends which give authenticity for this location. In the worship at Bethel a special significance was found in the fact that this ancient patriarch had experienced these revelations at just this place. Consequently Bethel came to hold a place of high importance among the old sanctuaries. During the period of the judges it attained a central place, supplanting Shechem in importance, as can be seen from the account of Samuel's yearly circuit culminating at this site (1 Sam. 7:16). Later, after the breakup of the united monarchy, Jeroboam was even able to capitalize on the long-established importance of this site by setting it up as a rival sanctuary to Jerusalem (1 Kings 12:29).

But what does the Bethel theophany imply for the Jacob narrative? Here, at some point, the tradition has interpreted it as the turning point where Jacob flees from Esau. In this sense, then, it underscores God's special care for the patriarch in the extenuating conditions following his rivalry with Esau, even though the deceitful character of Jacob seems to provide no problem for the divine protection promised in this tradition. But even this is not the end of the tradition's meaning. In the course of its development and use it comes to reach far beyond the relation between Jacob and Esau. Now the promise given to Jacob becomes part of a larger pledge which embraces also the descendants of the patriarch as well (Gen. 28:13–14). It is probably with the incorporation of such motifs that the latest meaning of the tradition is associated.

It is possible, therefore, to trace a certain development in the cultic importance of this site and tradition. To summarize, there is the connection of the site with Jacob, the particular role it came to play in the larger promise remembered by Israel, the character of some of the early Israelite cultic installations, and the explanation about the great pillar which later pilgrims to the site would have seen and possibly may also have poured libations upon. Finally, there is the interesting little notice in 28:22 of the presentation of the tenth, an act which many of those who later came to the site for worship must also have performed in imitation of the vow and offering attributed to the founding patriarch.

The rest of the theophanies occur after Jacob has spent long years in the territory of Laban. It might be noted that while he is in Laban's employ, no such divine encounters take place. The Jacob-Laban cycle is marked by a striking absence of any reference to the divine work. Following upon this cycle, however, divine appearances recur with regularity. The first two are localized in the Gileadite region east of the Jordan, at Mahanaim and Penuel. Of the first (Gen. 32:1–2), only the briefest remark is made, that, as the patriarch went on his way, he saw "the angels of God," and this led him to remark about the site, "This is God's army ($mah^an\bar{e}h$)!" Apparently the tradition has preserved here a further etiology of a site later important in the stories of David and Saul (2 Sam. 2:8–9; 17:24–27), but whose location has not yet been discovered. The name of the site, Mahanaim, suggests some association with Jacob's division of his company into two camps (32:7, $mah^an\bar{e}h$), as the wordplay suggests.

One of the most striking sections in the Jacob narrative as a whole is certainly the theophany connected with the site of Penuel (32:22–32). Gerhard von Rad has aptly written about this section: "In this narrative more than in any other of the ancient patriarchal traditions something of the long process of formation to which this material was subjected in history becomes clear. Many generations formed and interpreted it. It was in motion for centuries until it finally crystallized in the final form which it now possesses. This knowledge about such a long history is not, however, only a concern of a special science, but it concerns everyone who wants to understand the story; for only then can the reader be preserved from false expectations of a hasty search for 'the' meaning of this story. There are scarcely examples in Western literature of this kind of narrative, which combines such spaciousness in content with such stability in form."[13]

As we attempt to understand the Penuel theophany, therefore, it is important to remember that we are dealing throughout with a tradition which has been passed on by means of a very complicated process. It is not possible to recover the original setting and understanding of this narrative, although some dim shadows can still be seen of what the story must

13. Von Rad, *Genesis*, p. 314.

have been like at early stages of its telling. The motif was recalled and transmitted apparently by groups on the east side of the Jordan, thereafter finding its way into larger cycles of material regarding Jacob, and finally being incorporated as an element in the larger historical work of the Pentateuch.

The main motif of the tradition is the nocturnal combat between Jacob and "the man." Comparative religion offers parallels to this motif with accounts of battles between special men and demons carried on by night.[14] It is possible that in its earliest strata the tradition may have had such meaning, employing the theme of a fierce conflict between the remembered saint and supernatural powers. An interesting biblical analogy is found in Exodus 4:24–26, the story of Moses' journey back to Egypt. He also encounters a supernatural power and is nearly destroyed by it. In the further retelling and reshaping of the Penuel tradition, it is clear that the one with whom Jacob fights is no less than God himself, and that conflict now serves as the pivot of the whole episode, and all its tangents and extensions. In the passionate conflict which ensues, then, Jacob is seen to be somewhat successful in the battle with this night visitor, although the thigh of the patriarch is thrown out of place during the encounter.

Two etiologies are included in the complicated structure of this narrative. On the one hand, following the conflict, the name of Jacob is changed to Israel in 32:28. In the second place, the name of the site at which this grim event took place is given as Penuel ("face of God") in 32:30, because the patriarch had seen God "face to face." In each of these assertions we can see the reflection of tradition at work, both in the way that Jacob's struggle becomes representative of that of the people later on, as well as the way the site preserved in its very name the outline of this important episode. In 32:32 the P interpretation of the tradition went even farther to link certain Israelite habits of dietary abstention with the dislocation of the patriarch's thigh.

An important feature about this episode is the way it is related to its context. The most immediate context with which

14. Cf. Helmer Ringgren, *Israelite Religion*, trans. David E. Green (Philadelphia: Fortress Press, 1966), pp. 72–73.

it is connected is the Jacob-Esau cycle, and there it forms a thought-provoking addition to the theme of pursuit and danger. The nocturnal conflict, with all its serious meaning, dwarfs the fearful encounter with the approaching brother. But a larger context is supplied through the name change of Jacob to Israel, and here the tradition has incorporated a secondary, but no less important, etymology for the name Israel. The patriarch's experience is paradigmatic for Israel as a people. Fundamentally Israel is constituted as a people whose deepest meaning is found in her conflict and struggle with God. This dimension to the Penuel episode represents a back and forth movement not unlike that which redaction criticism has discovered in the Gospels.[15] There is an alternation between what this account might mean in reference to an individual, as well as its larger meaning in relation to the people of Israel and their history and destiny.

The last theophany occurs in relation to the site of Shechem, with a further connection to Bethel. Upon returning from the east, Jacob stops at Shechem in Genesis 33:18–20, purchasing there a plot of land on which he erects an altar for El, Elohe-Israel ("God, the God of Israel"). The description is brief and to the point, and no clues are given as to why Shechem was important for such an altar. It is interesting that the following chapter, with its theme of the seduction and rape of Dinah by Shechem, the son of Hamor, has been placed here following the notice of the construction of the altar at Shechem. Evidently this has occurred through the principle of association operating in the amalgamation of traditions deriving from different backgrounds.

The narrative in Genesis 35:1–15 has been the object of intensive study by scholars. It was Albrecht Alt who first proposed that this section may suggest the ritual of an ancient pilgrimage from Shechem to Bethel.[16] These two sites, both of central importance in the period of the Israelite settlement, were eventually to come into some competition with each

15. Norman Perrin, *What Is Redaction Criticism?* (Philadelphia: Fortress Press, 1969), pp. 45, 52.
16. Albrecht Alt, "Die Wallfahrt von Sichem nach Bethel," in *Kleine Schriften zur Geschichte des Volkes Israel* (München: C. H. Beck'sche Verlagsbuchhandlung, 1953), I: 79–88.

other. As an Israelite sanctuary, Shechem seems to be the earlier of the two, its place being taken somewhat later by Bethel. Martin Noth has even suggested that we must assume a certain amount of suppression of the traditions about Shechem in the light of the later sanctuary of Bethel, since a later shrine often tends to supplant traditions about an earlier site. In fact, Noth held the view that the Jacob traditions were originally localized at the site of Shechem, and only later were transferred to the Bethel sanctuary.[17] But it appears that the tradition had a specific intention in offering the appearance of God to Jacob at Bethel as the framework of the whole narrative. For it is just at this site that Jacob sets out in the time of his uncertainty, and it is to this place that he returns at the end. Apart from the brief notices of the trip to Ephrath (35:16–21), it is fundamentally with this narrative about Bethel that the Jacob cycle ends.

THE REDACTION OF THE MATERIALS

What we have found in this section, then, is a complex of material involving examples of saga and connected narrative, a number of oracles associated with divine appearances, as well as traditions which were probably employed to present and validate the history of several important sites and sanctuaries in ancient Israel. Regarding this material, traditio- and form critical examination shows that its earliest form consisted of largely independent units, preserved by groups or individuals belonging to the tribes of the central hill country, including the Gilead area east of the Jordan. Noth's suggestion that the large tribe of Ephraim had a special importance for this material is also worth considering. Such a background implies a certain diversity in the material, but this does not need to lead to an atomized understanding of it, a charge which is sometimes brought against traditio-historical method. Rather, if one conceives of the Jacob groups as being spread over a number of regions, as the biblical records themselves seem to indicate, then it is possible that certain traditions

17. Noth, *Überlieferungsgeschichte des Pentateuch*, pp. 86–95.

were carried on in some areas and others elsewhere. Such a recognition need not even prejudge the question of the historical validity of the material.

Following a time of rather independent development and transmission in the case of certain of the units of tradition, we can assume a period when similar types of material came to be collected into what have been called cycles, that is, compilations of material which could be brought together because of the similarity of motifs and interests. In the formation of the material such principles as that of association appear to have been at work. Further steps were taken as these various cycles of material were brought together to form a larger whole, and this may have begun to occur when some of the material was still in an oral stage. Finally, the latest compositional stages were reached when such large blocks of material were incorporated as part of a large historical work, such as that of J and eventually that of P, to which the fundamental material could be seen as related in new and meaningful ways. It is in this framework, then, that we find the broadest theology of Jacob as part of the continuous promise given to Israel from early times onward.

As we have proceeded, then, it has been possible to gain some insight into what some of the individual sagas involving Jacob intended to convey in their early usage. At this time they were often oral stories and their chief significance would be to stimulate the memory of certain groups about this ancestor. What is striking about these individual stories is that, by themselves, they are often characterized by a remarkable worldliness. The various units in the Jacob-Esau cycle portray dramatic scenes in which there is a contest of wits and in which certain things happen which even sound offensive.

However, as we have noted above, when these stories were joined with other elements, such as the theophanies, a deeper meaning emerged. Now the stories of Jacob's relations with Esau, on the one hand, and with Laban, on the other, are offered as episodes in which the patriarch is found in trying circumstances, sometimes for which he himself is to blame. In such extremities, however, the divine assurance is granted again and again to Jacob. All the so-called cult legends of the various sites at which appearances occur take up the motif of the divine pledge to Jacob.

In the tradition, then, the story of Jacob has come to take on several memorable meanings. On one side, the narrative highlights the theme of strife, which appears as a repeated refrain throughout—in the case of Jacob and Esau, Jacob and Laban, and finally Jacob and the one with whom he wrestles at Penuel. In their usage of this material, later Israelites would not fail to hear in it some audible sounds illuminating their own challenges. At the same time, the Jacob narrative is part of the larger theme of promise and fulfillment, which spans the history of the partiarchs. Although the promises to Jacob probably originally had a meaning in terms of a more immediate settlement of the early seminomadic peoples in the arable land, at a later age these traditions have been joined with the exodus and land allocation themes. In this manner, the Jacob narrative has become, in the end, a primary element in the great history of God's acts with Israel.

The history of tradition is also interested in how such materials and themes continue to be employed in later times. In the case of Jacob not a great deal is made of this tradition later, although the name of Jacob is found abundantly in the Old Testament. At many places in the Old Testament it became synonymous with Israel as a people, as suggested already in the traditions of the name change in the Jacob narrative itself. One interesting use of the old narrative traditions is found in Hosea 12:2–6. Here the patriarch's cunning is taken as a characteristic typical of north Israel's deceit, a kind of congenital defect of people in that region. As far as Hosea is concerned, the northern Israelites to whom he addresses his words appear almost to be a "chip off the old block." However, the special way that Jacob and God were bound together in their encounters is also noted, and this becomes the basis on which the prophet calls his people to a new kind of faithfulness and waiting on the Lord (Hos. 12:6).

IV

Tradition History
and the Prophets

When traditio-historical method is employed in the study of the prophetic books, new problems arise which are peculiar to this literature. It is instructive, therefore, to take as a further illustration of how this method works a selection from the prophetic writings. The particular section chosen is that part of the Book of Isaiah (Isa. 40–55) which is commonly called Second Isaiah, because it has long been recognized as dealing with a later period and different themes than the earlier part of this prophetic book. Second Isaiah confronts us with many interpretative problems, which are illuminated in an interesting way when examined from the perspective of the history of tradition.

TRANSMISSION PROBLEMS IN SECOND ISAIAH

A fundamental problem in Isaiah 40–55 is its relation to the Book of Isaiah as a whole. Earlier scholarship already perceived that a break occurs at the end of Isaiah 39. Beginning with Isaiah 40, the setting is no longer the late eighth century B.C. as it is for most of Isaiah 1–39, nor are the adversaries of Israel the Assyrians and Aramaeans as is the case in the first part of the book. Rather, the people have already passed through a devastating time of captivity. At the same time, the prophet goes so far as to suggest that their hope might lie in the sudden rise to power of Cyrus, who is even called the Lord's "anointed" (Isa. 44:28; 45:1). By means of such specific references, scholars concluded that we are dealing in Isaiah 40–55 with a different prophet from the earlier Isaiah, one who must have lived and preached during the latter years of the Jewish exile in Babylon. In addition, Isaiah 56–66 has been taken by some to represent the message of yet a third prophet, commonly referred to as Third Isaiah.

Such discussion points to basic questions in the interpretation of the Book of Isaiah. How have the several parts of this large prophetic book come together in their composition? If they do not all derive from the same prophet, how is their relation to each other to be explained? Source criticism, as applied to the prophets, performed the negative task of showing the differences between these two sections of the Book of Isaiah. It examined the divergences in vocabulary, form, and the ideological and thematic characteristics of the two parts, and demonstrated that these two sections of the book must derive from different hands. However, this criticism was unable to provide a satisfactory answer to the question of how this material from different periods could have been brought together into the large complex we now possess. Traditio-historical analysis has devoted itself to these same phenomena and has offered explanations of its own about the development of this material.

As it had done for the Pentateuch, history of tradition brought its interests in transmission and composition to bear upon prophetic books like Isaiah. In the first chapter we have noted that several scholars have assumed that the prophets were primarily speakers and not writers, and that their words passed through a primary stage of oral formation and delivery before they were set down in writing. Along with this, many tradition historians have worked with a conception of prophetic schools, or circles, which they have viewed as being closely associated with the prophet himself. These so-called pupils of the prophet were often with him when he spoke his words, were active in preserving them in their memory, and were finally responsible for putting them into the form in which we now have them.

There seems to be evidence for the existence of such groups in the Old Testament, although there is a problem as to whether such followers of the prophets were as important for the composition of these books as some tradition historians have made them. Nevertheless, there is the interesting account of Jeremiah's scribe, Baruch, who is said to have written down the words of the well-known prophet (Jer. 36:1–4). A further verse, frequently appealed to, is Isaiah 8:16, where the words of Isaiah of Jerusalem are said to be bound up and sealed among his disciples. Some tradition historians have taken the word "disciple" in this verse as conclusive evidence for a circle of followers of Isaiah, but it should be pointed out that this interpretation has not gone unchallenged.[1] If it is interpreted in the former way, then it can be argued that these persons were placed in charge of the prophet's words until the time would arrive when they could be put at the disposal of everyone.

Taking such conclusions and applying them to the compositional problems of the Book of Isaiah, tradition historians have proposed that the relation of the various components of this book is to be explained by means of the existence of both an earlier prophet and later disciples and successors who have followed in the earlier Isaiah's steps. Thus, the anonymous prophet, Second Isaiah, is viewed as a later disciple of the Isaiah school and he is interpreted as being indebted to various beliefs and ideas of the earlier prophet. For both the earlier and later Isaiah there is a burning interest in Zion and in the centrality of Jerusalem in the purpose of God. Both are also interested in the traditions of David preserved at Jerusalem, as well as in the kingship of Yahweh. At the same time, new motifs have arisen with Second Isaiah as over against those of his predecessor. The important point, however, is the way this approach attempts to explain the special character of this prophetic work, as well as its relation to the earlier part of the book.

THE PROPHETS AND TRADITION

Although Wellhausen's contributions to Old Testament study did not concentrate on the prophets, his work on the religion of Israel provided the impetus for others to undertake a similar interpretation of the prophets. Wellhausen had de-

1. See the remarks of Georg Fohrer, *Introduction to the Old Testament*, trans. David E. Green (Nashville: Abingdon Press, 1968), pp. 40, 359.

scribed Old Testament religion as a development from simple, close-to-nature religious experience to the more complex practice of later priestly religion. This interpretation was modeled on the scheme of evolutionary progress prominent in nineteenth century thought.[2] What is important for a study of the prophets is that an analogous kind of interpretation was applied to them, in which they came to be viewed as representing the highest stage of Old Testament religion. An important scholar who advanced such a view was Bernhard Duhm, who interpreted the prophets as great individualists capable of leaving such things as cult and sacrifices behind them, and who strove for a higher religion grounded in ethics. Viewed in this manner, the prophets bore witness to a new flourishing of moral sensitivity unparalleled in Israel's earlier religious practices and traditions. For this reason, too, they were thought to have largely broken with earlier tradition, and such oracles as the "anti-cultic passages" in Amos 5:21–24 and Isaiah 1:12–17, were taken as evidence for the radical departure of the prophetic movement from tradition. Such an interpretation was prominent at the end of the nineteenth and beginning of the twentieth century.[3]

Just as subsequent study has challenged Wellhausen's interpretation of the development of Israelite religion, so traditio-historical and form critical study of the prophets has brought a necessary revision of prophetic interpretation which followed similar lines, such as that of Duhm. In fact, the work which has been done with such concentration on the earlier traditions of Israel is only now being seen in relation to the later prophetic literature, and this is resulting in new perspectives on the various prophets.[4] The problem narrows itself down to a rather simple formulation: Are the prophets to be envisioned as having broken completely with past tradition and leaving

2. George E. Mendenhall, "Biblical History in Transition," in *The Bible and the Ancient Near East,* Essays in Honor of William Foxwell Albright, ed. G. Ernest Wright (Garden City: Doubleday & Co., 1961), p. 36.

3. See Bernhard Duhm, *Israels Propheten* (Tübingen: J. C. B. Mohr [Paul Siebeck], 1916), pp. 3–8.

4. For an introduction to the problems of the relation of the prophets to older tradition, with special emphasis on Hosea, see Walter Brueggemann, *Tradition for Crisis: A Study in Hosea* (Richmond: John Knox Press, 1968).

it behind them as they developed a new message? Or are they in any sense rooted in the old traditions? And, if they are, how do they speak out of these to address themselves to the new events of their age? These questions are of such foundatiqnal significance that they cannot be answered without a restudy of the prophetic literature, and such work is going on with great vitality at the present time. Simple answers, of course, are not possible, since there is a newness in the prophets which cannot be accounted for by recourse to the older tradition. At the same time, it is increasingly evident that all the prophets in one way or another speak in a form, and with a content, that makes their attachment to these traditions unmistakable.

In no other prophet, perhaps, is this grounding in the old traditions so apparent and so lively as is the case with Second Isaiah. Illustrations of this could extend the present work beyond its necessary limits. For the purposes of making the point we confine ourselves to three aspects of the message of Second Isaiah, each of which reflects the relation of this prophet's message to earlier traditions of Israel.

SECOND ISAIAH AND THE SALVATION ORACLE

The first example of the way Second Isaiah relates to older traditions has to do with a characteristic form of some of the oracles found in this book. Of the various types of oracles which form criticism has isolated in this prophet, one which is of special significance is the "salvation oracle," the *Heilsorakel* of German Old Testament scholarship. It was Gunkel's student, Joachim Begrich, who did a thorough analysis of the salvation oracle in Second Isaiah.[5]

The sections in Second Isaiah to which Begrich gave his attention were: Isaiah 41:8–13, 41:14–16; 43:1–3a, 5; 44:2–5; 48:17–19; 49:7, 14–15; 51:7–8; and 54:4–8. The most striking thing about all these oracles is their common pattern, which Begrich's analysis showed to contain the following elements. In the first place, the oracle usually begins with a formula, "Do not fear." This is followed by the naming of the one who is being addressed, and sometimes certain epithets indicating

5. Joachim Begrich, "Das priesterliche Heilsorakel," *Zeitschrift für die alttestamentliche Wissenschaft* 52 (1934), pp. 81–92.

the relationship between God and the addressee are attached to his name. In the third place, then, a declaration is made, giving assurance of the nearness of Yahweh to the one who is being addressed. Often this is in the form of a first person assurance such as "for I will be with you," or "I am your helper." Finally, an announcement is made of the ways in which God intends to carry out his promises of assistance. Not all of these elements are found each time in the various oracles, but this is taken as the full, "pure" form, which does occur several times (e.g., Isa. 41:8–13).

The arresting thing about these oracles is the way their language corresponds to that of certain of the laments which are spoken from the other side, that is, from people petitioning God rather than vice versa. A particularly good example of this is the complaint in Psalm 22:6: "But I am a worm, and no man." Corresponding to this are the words of the oracle in Isaiah 41:14: "Fear not, you worm Jacob." But this is just one example which is adduced by Begrich to support his thesis. He cites other instances which show that the correspondence between laments and the salvation oracle is too pronounced to admit of any other explanation than that there must have been some relation between them. One passage noted by Begrich even becomes explicit in this interrelationship of the two. Lamentations 3:57 contains the grateful words of the supplicant who says:

> Thou didst come near when I called on thee:
> thou didst say, "Do not fear!"

Begrich's argument, then, is that this must explain why some of the laments of the Old Testament witness to a change of mood which sometimes occurs toward the end of the prayer. In some prayers (e.g., Ps. 6:9–10), the tone of the petitioning may turn abruptly from lament to expressions of confidence that God has responded. The explanation for this must lie in the announcement of an oracle of deliverance and assurance which must have intervened. The person who pronounced such a word would probably have been a priest, and this is why Begrich and others came to designate this oracle type as a "priestly" salvation oracle.

The importance of this discovery, which has met widespread acceptance among students of the Old Testament, lies in the way in which it illuminates not only the cult of old Israel, but also a prophetic book like that of Second Isaiah. The prominence of this very form indicates that Second Isaiah builds his message, at least in part, on older conventional formulae which were at home in Israel's cultic practices. The prophet has, of course, set them in a broader framework in his message. Nevertheless, the *Heilsorakel* form provides for him the shape in which his far-flung promises of hope and expectation for the exiles are stated.

This example of a conventional pattern of lament followed by an oracle of assurance means that Second Isaiah is rooted in a certain usage of older traditions. It also means that a prophet like Second Isaiah not only knew certain patterns from the older cultus, but also employed them as a fundamental form for his own message. Two points consequently follow from this fact. In the first place, such a use of old forms provides evidence of how one prophet does not break with ancient tradition, but stands in continuity with it, even though his message witnesses to new aspects of God's work. Secondly, this use of older, familiar forms would have made his message that much more understandable to his listeners. If we can generalize at this point, the prophets spoke by means of patterns with which the people were familiar, and their usage of themes which were commonly known from the traditions would have provided a clarity and immediateness to their proclamations.

SECOND ISAIAH AND THE EXODUS

Naturally a theme as central as that of the exodus is to be found in many places in the Old Testament. Various prophets make their appeal to it and build their challenges to Israel on it. Confessionally the exodus is the beginning of Israel. It was the act of divine benefaction which formed and sustained Israel's faith. And her own vocation was one of continued faithfulness based upon this act of gracious emancipation from her bondage.

63

As commentators on Second Isaiah have frequently noted, the exodus theme is the most prominent of all the ancient traditions to which Second Isaiah is related.[6] But what is of special importance is the manner in which this prophet takes up this old theme and uses it as the essential image of his vision and proclamation about the future. A number of significant studies of the theme of a "new exodus" have been presented in recent years, devoted to examining the way this prophet interprets this older tradition in relation to the new events he discerns in the present and anticipates in the future.[7]

The deportation of part of the Judean population to Babylon in the early sixth century B.C. called for meaningful and decisive interpretation. The destructive events of 587 B.C., and those which immediately preceded and followed, represented to many the collapse of nearly all that had provided the hope and ground of the old faith. It was into such a setting that Second Isaiah spoke his message. Confronted with the challenges of this period, the prophet could have followed several options. He could have voiced despair in the face of these events. Along with this, he might have sounded the note of the futility of any recollection of the past sacred history. That such options were considered by some in the exile seems to be indicated by various references in the book of Second Isaiah itself. The prophet, however, was led a different way, one which neither abandoned nor attempted to repristinate the ancient tradition.

Schooled as he was in the old traditions, Second Isaiah reached to them for the basis and starting point of his own message. This is clear in 40:3 where the theme taken up is that of a going out or departure, in which the divine glory will be seen "in the wilderness." In 40:10 it is the "arm" of the Lord which is about to demonstrate its power and rule, one of the favorite exodus metaphors in the old tradition (Exod.

6. Gerhard von Rad, *Old Testament Theology*, trans. D. M. G. Stalker, 2 vols. (New York: Harper & Row, 1962, 1965), II:239.

7. See especially Bernhard W. Anderson, "Exodus Typology in Second Isaiah," in *Israel's Prophetic Heritage*, Essays in Honor of James Muilenburg, ed. B. W. Anderson and W. Harrelson (New York: Harper & Bros., 1962), pp. 177–95; Joseph Blenkinsopp, "Scope and Depth of Exodus Tradition in Deutero-Isaiah 40–55," in *The Dynamism of Biblical Tradition*, Concilium, vol. 20 (New York: Paulist Press, 1967), pp. 41–50.

15:16). And in 40:11 the description is of the tender care with which Yahweh will feed, gather, and lead his flock. As von Rad has pointed out, this stress on God himself leading out the people stands in contrast with the haste with which the first exodus was made.[8] In 52:12 it is even stated that the people will not go out the same way this time, since God will be leading them directly and will protect them from the rear.

Perhaps the key description is found in 43:14–21, where Yahweh is about to send to Babylon to break the power of those who hold the captives in bondage. Verse 15 of this section contains a self-predication typical of the exodus recital elsewhere in the older traditions, such as in Exodus 20:2. Here the form is "I am Yahweh, your holy One." The imagery becomes explicit in its reiteration of old exodus themes in verses 16–17. God is one "who makes a way in the sea, a path in the mighty waters." And even more reminiscent of that tradition is the language of 43:17:

> who brings forth chariot and horse,
>   army and warrior;
> they lie down, they cannot rise,
>   they are extinguished, quenched
>   like a wick.

In chapter 48, one of the important sections on the contrast between the "former" and the "latter" things, there is further allusion to the exodus imagery. Yahweh has tried his people "in the furnace of affliction" in 48:10, a technical phrase for the stay in Egypt. And in 48:20–22 the people are commanded to "go out!" Here the verb $y\bar{a}tz\bar{a}'$ is used, the very verb which is a *terminus technicus* for the exodus elsewhere (e.g., Exod. 20:2). Finally, in 50:2, it is recalled that Yahweh is one who can dry up the sea and the rivers, resulting in the stink of dead fish—an adaptation of the pollution of the Nile theme from the plague traditions. And in 51:9–11, a motif also associated with the exodus, but which has an even older history going back into the mythology of Canaan, is employed. Here God is called upon as the one who cut Rahab into pieces and made the sea dry to its depths, that the redeemed ones might pass through it.

8. Von Rad, *Old Testament Theology*, II:246.

How, then, does Second Isaiah employ these old exodus traditions which are diffused through so many of the oracles of this book? In the first place, it is the exodus traditions which supply many of the figures which the prophet draws upon, as well as the language in which he sets forth his own proclamation. Similarly, it is the way God is remembered as working in the ancient deliverance that provides for the prophet the new word about how he promises to act in the near future. Here are the forceful symbols and the dynamic language which can be opened up once more in a time of crisis. Secondly, the prophet does not simply reinforce these images in their old meanings, but the language and recollection of the exodus reveal incomparably new expectations about the future work of God with his people.

It is this last point which is indicated in the prophet's contrast between the "former things" and the "latter things." There can be little doubt that this contrast points to some important, and even central, aspects of Second Isaiah's message. Old Testament scholarship has not yet reached a consensus on just what the intent of this language is in the various places where it occurs. In spite of this, it appears that part of what the former things is referring to, in any case, is the great prior act of deliverance in the exodus from Egypt. The prophet has no intention of minimizing the magnitude of that event. He goes on to proclaim, however, that what is about to happen in the divine working will be, by comparison, something even more stupendous than the original exodus. Such a coming salvation invites the listeners to look, not backwards in simple memory, but with concentrated anticipation of the future, in which wholly uncontemplated events are about to take place.

> Remember not the former things,
> nor consider the things of old.
> Behold, I am doing a new thing;
> now it springs forth, do you not
> perceive it?
> I will make a way in the wilderness
> and rivers in the desert (Isa. 43:18–19).

The usage of the old exodus imagery by Second Isaiah does not result in a facile attempt simply to restore old traditions. Rather, the traditions of the exodus open the way to expectations of the future. They free men from the past rather than require them to emulate it. The old traditions carry along potent symbols on the basis of which further divine revelation can be disclosed. The God of the exodus is not one who is withdrawn, having done his onetime act of redemption in the past. He lives on, actively meeting his people in times of new challenge which call for their response. A new time, according to the prophet, is on the brink of appearing. It will overshadow even the greatness of the former saving events, making them small by contrast. The epitome of this new deliverance will be known in the form of a new "going out," a new exodus.

Thus the exodus language here has been transposed into a new and higher key, as Bernhard Anderson has put it.[9] But the question is whether Second Isaiah has done something which is completely novel in his usage of the old traditions. The answer is that actually the prophet is following in a type of interpretation which is at home in the Old Testament as a whole. Such interpretation did not simply carry along the recollection of older events and memories, but brought them always vitally into touch with the contemporary challenges of the divine activity. This kind of reactualization, as it is often called today, can be found in such works as the Deuteronomic History. We have already noted it, to some degree, in the way that the various Jacob traditions are handled in the later building up of that narrative. However, it is certainly true that Second Isaiah has intensified this process of reinterpretation. For him the old exodus language takes on an almost eschatologized meaning. The new "going out" which the prophet announces belongs to an event and age of unparalleled and seemingly final salvation. It is this special use of the old language and descriptions that sets Second Isaiah's message apart as a unique proclamation.

9. Anderson, "Exodus Typology in Second Isaiah," p. 191.

Thus Old Testament interpretation has recovered some valuable insights in this case by an attention to the history of tradition. Such study has made it possible to take up again the whole problem of typology in the Old Testament, but in a new way. During the nineteenth century especially, classical typological interpretation of the Old Testament suffered a serious blow at the hands of critical study. Following this, such interpretation decreased in importance and became virtually extinct in many quarters. However, the kind of traditio-historical study as that devoted to Second Isaiah has opened up the problem in a new way. Here we apparently have a lively form of typological thinking in the way the prophet uses the old exodus motifs. At the same time, what is clear in such usage is how deeply rooted this interpretation is in the understanding of the older divine work in history. The prophet does not employ typological connections in a schematic way, divesting them of their historical rootedness. Rather, he knows the power of the old revelations, employs their language, suggests new and futurist dimensions through them, and is able to pass on beyond them to anticipate the new divine activity about to occur.

SECOND ISAIAH AND THE CREATION TRADITIONS

Probably no aspect of Second Isaiah's message is so immediately evident as the way he weaves into his theology the motif of creation. Along with sections of the Primeval History (Gen. 1–11) and some of the psalms emphasizing nature, it is in Second Isaiah that creation is employed most prominently in the Old Testament. Such a situation again raises important questions. How is the sudden appearance of such a strong use of creation in this prophet to be explained? How does he employ such motifs in relation to others which are present in his message? And, how does Second Isaiah's use of creation relate to traditions of creation known elsewhere both in the Bible and in extrabiblical literature? Probably none of these questions can be responded to with certainty at this point, but it is possible to suggest some answers to them.

The first thing to be recognized in the creation declarations of Second Isaiah is the diversity of settings in which they are found. At the beginning of Second Isaiah's prophecy we find the creation motif introduced in the form of a challenging question, which is certainly meant to suggest that the answer to this rhetorical utterance must be that God's power is insurmountable.

> Who has measured the waters in the hollow of his hand
>   and marked off the heavens with a span,
> enclosed the dust of the earth in a measure
>   and weighed the mountains in scales? (Isa. 40:12).

This same kind of disputational form of speech characterizes the moving speech by God the Creator in Job 38. Another favorite mode of expression, different from but also reminiscent of the disputation question, is the usage of a participial phrase to characterize God's power as creator. In 40:22 God is "he who stretches out the heavens like a curtain."

In other sections of Second Isaiah the motif of creation is used along with depictions which may be called eschatological, such as those in 41:17–20, 43:16–21, and 42:14–17. Here descriptions of the wilderness as experiencing transformation are part of the promise of future salvation. Since nature itself participates in the eschatological salvation, a new kind of song is also commanded to be sung. The various parts of nature are invited to "sing to Yahweh," such as is done in 42:10–13, 45:8, 49:13, 52:9, and 54:1–3. Another song, or at least declaration, is related to older Canaanite motifs. It calls upon Yahweh to awaken as in the times of old when he slew Rahab (51:9–11), clearly now a motif centering in the exodus, as we have seen.

Still other creation declarations are found in other settings. Isaiah 42:5, 43:1, 45:18, 51:13, and 51:15–16, are all descriptions which serve as epithets of the power and sovereignty of Yahweh. In 44:24–28 and 48:12–13 the creation motif is taken up as part of the self-predication of God. Closely related are the divine assertions that various things were made by God, in 45:7 and 45:11–13. Finally, one usage which occurs several times is the assertion that what God does will outlast the vanishing creation. Such an intention is found in 40:6–8, 51:6, and 54:10.

The variety of uses to which the theme is put by this prophet shows how fundamentally he has woven it into his message at almost all points. Yet, as several scholars who have studied the problem have shown, creation in Second Isaiah does not stand as an independent motif. Von Rad was the first to offer a specific interpretation in which creation in Second Isaiah was said to be dependent on the more elementary theme of the election of Israel.[10] Thus the celebration of creation called for in so many ways in this prophet's message serves to heighten his expectation and joy over the continuance of Israel's election and her future preservation. Although this interpretation can be disputed, it does find some basis in such passages as 43:1, where the creation language ("I formed," etc.) is used, above all, for the origins of Israel. Apart from this, however, it is evident that Second Isaiah's message receives a decidedly comprehensive thrust through the usage of this motif.

In introducing the motif of creation as strongly as he does, Second Isaiah is not simply inventing something new which is unknown before. The usage to which he puts it in his distinctive way is new. At the same time, he has apparently drawn on older traditions of creation which were available to him. Where are these to be found? In the first place, it is evident that there is an impressive connection between Second Isaiah's message and the psalms. We have already noted a relation between these two sections of the Old Testament in the salvation oracle form which was given as a response to a lamentation. In addition to this, much of the tone of Second Isaiah is characterized by praise and exultation.[11] Such jubilation is given expression in a language which frequently parallels that of the psalms, and at some points close resemblances can

10. Gerhard von Rad, "Das theologische Problem des alttestamentliche Schöpfungsglaubens," in *Gesammelte Studien zum Alten Testament*, Theologische Bücherei, no. 8 (München: Christian Kaiser Verlag, 1961), pp. 136–47. The article appeared originally in 1936 and has now been translated into English as "The Theological Problem of the Old Testament Doctrine of Creation," in Gerhard von Rad, *The Problem of the Hexateuch and Other Essays*, trans. E. W. T. Dicken (New York: McGraw-Hill, 1966), pp. 131–43.
11. See Claus Westermann, *Isaiah 40–66*, trans. D. M. G. Stalker (Philadelphia: Westminster Press, 1969), p. 14.

be seen between this prophet's message and the psalms of the "new song" (Pss. 96–98; cf. Isa. 42:10).

This undoubtedly means that Second Isaiah was familiar with the traditions of worship and praise found in the psalms. Although it is not necessary to go so far as to view the prophet as a cultic functionary in the technical sense, at the same time it is evident that his message is shaped by his acquaintance with the language and expressions of such worship. But a further observation must be made. Not only is the prophet steeped in the psalms, but he also seems to be drawing on other older traditions. It is noteworthy that the Hebrew root for "create" (*bārā'*), which is such an evident element in the P narrative of creation (Gen. 1:1–2:4a), is a recurring term in Second Isaiah (e.g., Isa. 40:26, 28; 42:5). We may not be far wrong, then, to suggest that Second Isaiah has taken up the particular traditions of creation, such as in the Pentateuch and the psalms, and has used them brilliantly in describing the extensive scope of God's activity.

The problem as to what factors moved the prophet to take up the creation motif in this way is not easily solved. Different efforts have been made to asnwer this question. Engnell advanced the interpretation that the prophet demonstrated a close acquaintance with sacral kingship in his messianic utterances, and it would follow from this view that the great blocks of creation tradition may have passed into his message under this influence.[12] Others have suggested that Second Isaiah's contacts with the Babylonians catalyzed this interest in the creation traditions, especially since the Babylonians possessed their own creation traditions, and the latter may have stimulated the development of belief about Yahweh as creator. Still others have pointed to the crisis of the exile as provoking an expanded understanding of Yahweh's lordship. Such points will continue to be debated. But what seems clear is that Second Isaiah is one of the first to have used these traditions to proclaim the work of Yahweh as an arch stretching over creation, history, and eschatological fulfillment.[13]

12. Ivan Engnell. "The Ebed Yahweh Songs and the Suffering Messiah in Deutero-Isaiah," *Bulletin of the John Rylands Library* 31 (1948): 54–93.
13. Fohrer, *Introduction to the Old Testament*, pp. 383–84.

V

Traditio-Historical
Method and Theology

Those interested in analyzing the consequences of traditio-historical method for the theology of the Old Testament have a significant source book readily at hand. The two-volume work on Old Testament theology by Gerhard von Rad, to which reference has been made several times in this book, represents a comprehensive effort to write a theology of the Old Testament in a framework of traditio-historical investigation.[1] In addition, smaller monographs have been appearing which have also illuminated the special contributions to theological understanding which the use of these methods is making.

For von Rad, the matters discussed in this book are not merely peripheral. It is in the traditio-historical process itself that he sees the seeds of an Old Testament theology. That is, Old Testament theology arises from Israel's own way of receiving and responding to the words and deeds of God. This process, by which older themes about the ways of God with Israel are taken up and seen in new ways at a later time, points the way to understanding the Old Testament's own confessions of God. Thus theological study of the Old Testament ought not to see its primary task as synthesizing and then abstracting certain Old Testament conceptions of God, man, and redemption. It ought rather to concentrate its attention directly on the process by which the confessions of God's words and deeds are conveyed from generation to generation. That is,

1. Gerhard von Rad, *Old Testament Theology*, trans. D. M. G. Stalker, 2 vols. (New York: Harper & Row, 1962, 1965).

72

Old Testament theology will be implicit in the very study of the intricate problems of transmission of the traditions themselves. Von Rad's work provides an impressive illustration of such an approach.

Von Rad's contention is that in the Old Testament the confession of Yahweh's deeds does not come to an end.[2] There is an ever new history which is taken up afresh and interpreted. It is not as though Israel has a memory of the past which is finally completed, although there is certainly the recognition that particular events are unique and normative. But this does not turn the present into a mere appendage to older, more powerful events. Rather, men are invited to see the continuing activity of God in each new present. And this they do by recalling those events in the past which have proven themselves to be of revelatory power. Thus, we have seen that the exodus tradition is not carried along simply as a historical memory. This very theme is opened up in its continuing power and meaning as it illuminates later experiences.

This characteristic, of taking old traditions and interpreting them in relation to later events, is integral to the Old Testament's own proclamation. Study of the Old Testament today is showing more and more how such a spirit was at work, and we have noted several examples in the preceding chapters. Neither the motifs of the patriarchs, the exodus, nor the wilderness, are allowed to stand without an extension of their significance for Israel. Thus she continues to bear these themes along in new settings, and even the prophets are deeply grounded in them, in spite of all the newness of their proclamation. The task of a traditio-historical analysis is to follow this step-by-step process, all the while recognizing that such processes were carried out under a deep faith in the continuing work of God with Israel.

This approach to Old Testament theological problems, evidenced in von Rad's work, raises important questions which should be considered at this point. Most significant is the simple question: Is von Rad's effort to do a theology of the Old Testament in this way justified? Can it really be called a

2. Ibid., I:112.

theology of the Old Testament? Since its first appearance in German and its subsequent translation into English, this Old Testament theology has been the subject of considerable debate. Not a few have been critical of von Rad's procedure and have stated their preferences for the more traditional approach of treating Old Testament theology under such classical headings as God, man, and salvation.[3]

In a recent essay Roland de Vaux discussed the distinction between particular methods and contributions of different people working on the literature of the Old Testament.[4] The first is the historian who views the Old Testament as simply another historical document along with other documents from the various peoples of the ancient Near East. A second is the historian of religions. He also is interested in the Old Testament from a historical viewpoint, but primarily from the standpoint of what it can contribute to his interest in the specifically religious phenomena. Finally there is the theologian of the Old Testament. And here de Vaux recognized a definite confessional commitment which accompanies the study of the Old Testament by the theologian. Although the latter may use the results of other types of study, his work is different in that for him the Old Testament is the word of his own God. Therefore, he is looking to find what it can present to him for his own faith and that of the community to whom he delivers his study. Concerning von Rad, de Vaux noted that the latter's work more properly fits the category of a history of Israel's religion than a theology of the Old Testament.[5]

On the one hand, it is probably true that von Rad's Old Testament theology has introduced a certain one-sidedness into the subject. At the same time, the judgment that his work does not correspond to a theology of the Old Testament appears to be too limited an assessment. If one searches for analogies in other areas of theological study, von Rad's work might be said to be parallel to a study in historical theology.

3. So Robert Dentan, *Preface to Old Testament Theology*, rev. ed. (New York: Seabury Press, 1963), pp. 80, 119.
4. Roland de Vaux, "Method in the Study of Early Hebrew History," in *The Bible in Modern Scholarship*, ed. J. Philip Hyatt (Nashville: Abingdon Press, 1965), pp. 15–17.
5. Ibid., p. 16, n. 1.

In other words, his effort at following the reinterpretation of
traditions appears very much like the study of that process of
continuing exegesis of the Scriptures which Gerhard Ebeling
has suggested is a fundamental element in the study of church
history.[6] Such an approach recognizes the presence of
exegesis and interpretation already in the biblical literature
itself. Consequently, von Rad seems to be acting as neither
the historian of the ancient Near East nor the historian of religions, but rather as the historian of the proclamation which
Israel continues to make about God in her own continuing
exegesis of his works. In this sense a different description of
his effort might be useful, something like "a historical theology
of the Old Testament."

Apart from these misgivings, the theological importance of
traditio-historical study can be seen in a number of ways. The
first is that such work has allowed for a new appreciation of
the way in which ancient Israel saw her history. Somewhere
in the course of time there appeared an awareness which came
to be assumed in the way Israel handled her traditions.[7] Such
an assumption conceived of events as being connected with
each other, that what was experienced in an earlier event had
a continuity with something which occurred later. Israel's
sense of election and living under divine promise provided
the basis for such an interpretation of events. And, whereas it
may be true that such a viewpoint is not entirely unique to
the Israelites in the ancient Near Eastern world, it also seems
that no people made use of this mode of interpretation with
such fervor as did the people of the Old Testament.[8]

Closely related to such an interpretation of history is the
way events took on paradigmatic significance in the Old Testament. We have observed above how traditio-historical study
has brought with it a new awareness of typology in biblical
interpretation. Thus, it is common practice today to refer to
the "exodus typology" or "wilderness typology," without the

6. Gerhard Ebeling, *The Word of God and Tradition*, trans. S. H. Hooke
(Philadelphia: Fortress Press, 1968), pp. 11–31.
7. Von Rad, *Old Testament Theology*, II:105–6.
8. For a corrective to an overemphasis on the historical medium for
revelation in the Old Testament, see Bertil Abrektson, *History and the
Gods* (Lund: Gleerup, 1967).

stigma of an older inadequate use of typology being attached to this. The newer understanding of typology grows out of an empirical study of Israel's own way of seeing her history. Far from being an artificial imposition on the texts, it is just this notion of Israel's own comprehension of the typological power within events and experiences that has brought with it new perspectives on the message of the Old Testament.

One implication of this for Christian interpretation is that it has reopened the problem of the relation between the Old Testament and the New Testament.[9] It is noteworthy that the latter part of von Rad's second volume is devoted to the implications of traditio-historical method and typological interpretation for the relation of the testaments.[10] Such discussions appear to make von Rad's contention a just one, that not only should the Old Testament be understood by Christians from a perspective which takes the New Testament seriously, it should also be examined for what it has to say about the Christian's understanding of Jesus.

Two further ideas of theological importance are brought into clearer focus by traditio-historical study. On the one hand, traditio-historical study has implications for the understanding of revelation in the Old Testament. Revelation is in the very process by which Israel remembers, for it is in remembering that her identity in the present becomes continuously opened up to her. By means of a historical memory which reactualizes significant events of the past, she perceives the grounding for her life and her sense of vocation.[11] At the same time, along with such implications for revelation, there is the role that tradition plays in the formation and continuation of the Old Testament community. In its own way, traditio-historical examination shows how the continued recapitulation of testimony makes it possible for a community to move into new times and experiences which are still characterized by the

9. See the two collections of essays which take up many of these problems in Claus Westermann, ed., *Essays on Old Testament Hermeneutics* (Richmond: John Knox Press, 1963), and Bernhard W. Anderson, ed., *The Old Testament and Christian Faith* (New York: Harper & Row, 1963).

10. Von Rad, *Old Testament Theology*, II:319–35.

11. See on this Gerhard Gloege, *Offenbarung und Überlieferung* (Hamburg: Evangelischer Verlag, 1954), especially pp. 23–28.

power of revelation. Revelation, tradition, and community thus become a triad of interpenetrating actions and forces.

There is considerable significance in such discussion for the issues that theology faces as it attempts to interpret the meaning of faith in the present. On one side, theology has to come to grips with a great number of forces and influences in contemporary culture. At the same time, it finds itself dealing with the problems of the continuing significance of the testimonies which it has received from the community of the past. Thus both past testimony and present challenge are brought into tension with each other.

At this point theology can sometimes find assistance from various scholars outside its field. For instance, Hans-Georg Gadamer has called attention to the importance of tradition for the problem of knowledge in general. His contention is that the human being grasps the world through a language which has been transmitted to him and by means of inherited thought patterns in which the problems of life are framed. And thus, rather than minimizing the role that tradition plays in understanding, Gadamer affirms it as a necessary element in the hermeneutical process. The bulk of his study is devoted to the larger framework and structure of knowledge. Thus, as he views it, a large part of our life experience is found in the tension between what we carry over from the past and the new demands and insights which emerge from the present.[12]

Given the force of such observations, it is not surprising that the history of biblical interpretation and theology has found itself perennially in touch with the dynamics of tradition. In one way or another, much of contemporary theological effort is engaged in interpreting present experience with the help of biblical and churchly tradition. This reactualization of tradition takes place in many different ways. The attempts to communicate the continuing power of the biblical images through preaching, teaching, the various media, the arts, or drama, are involved in such dynamics. Celebrations of worship, which re-present the remembered themes of faith, point to a similar effort. It is just here that perspectives derived from traditio-historical study of the Old Testament probably have their greatest significance for theology and church life.

12. Hans-Georg Gadamer, *Wahrheit und Methode*, 2d ed. (Tübingen: J. C. B. Mohr [Paul Siebeck], 1965).

Glossary

'AM HÂ' ĀRETZ—Hebrew phrase for "the people of the land," possibly referring earlier to a class of land owners (2 Kings 21:24), while later it came to refer to the poor classes of society.

AMPHICTYONY—A federation of cities or tribes bound together for political, defensive, or religious purposes. In Old Testament study the term is commonly used for Israel's early social, political, and religious formation.

CULT—The public worship of a people, embracing customary forms, rites, feasts, times, places, and functionaries, as well as the common recollection (cult myth) which unites the gathered assembly in its worship.

ELOHIST—One of the "sources" discovered by source critics of the Pentateuch, commonly abbreviated E.

ESCHATOLOGY—The study of the last things, or events, at the end of time. Although debatable whether the term is apt in the prophets or not, it is often used to refer to the vision of the future depicted in their oracles.

ETIOLOGY—A story or narrative explaining the circumstances surrounding the origin of an institution, custom, human condition, or the name of a site.

FORM CRITICISM—The study of the development of literary types such as laws, oracles, love songs, fables, legends, laments, etc., and their life settings.

ORACLE—A divinely inspired message given in the form of an utterance by a priest or prophet.

PENTATEUCH—The first five books of the Old Testament.

REDACTION CRITICISM—The study of the process by which a redactor employs already existent oral and written material

78

and presents it in a particular theological or ideological framework.

RE-PRESENTATION—The dynamics involved in Israel's memory of her past in preaching and cultic enactment.

SITZ IM LEBEN—German expression meaning "setting in life," referring to the efforts of form critics to determine the life settings of particular literary types.

SOURCE CRITICISM—Sometimes called literary or documentary criticism, the method used by Old Testament critics in separating literary strands in the Pentateuch like those of the Yahwist and Elohist.

STYLE—Identifiable features in a particular author or tradition, such as vocabulary or distinctive syntax; for example, the Deuteronomic style.

THEME—The recollection of a past occurrence significant enough to be transmitted as a paradigm to later generations, often being brought into conjunction with similar or contrasting themes.

TYPOLOGY—The manner in which earlier events, personages, or institutions, are seen to be recapitulated in new ways at a later time.

YAHWIST—A further "source" discovered by critics in the Pentateuch, commonly abbreviated J.

Annotated Bibliography

GENERAL WORKS

The Dynamism of Biblical Tradition. Concilium, vol. 20. New York: Paulist Press, 1967. Contains essays by Roman Catholic scholars on the formation of biblical traditions.

KAISER, OTTO and KÜMMEL, WERNER G. *Exegetical Method: A Student's Handbook.* Translated with Introduction by E. V. N. Goetchius. New York: Seabury Press, 1967. This small paperback manual has excellent suggestions for method and interpretation, and contains, among others, helpful descriptions of traditio-historical method.

KOCH, KLAUS. *The Growth of the Biblical Tradition: The Form-Critical Method.* 2d German ed. translated by S. M. Cupitt. New York: Charles Scribner's Sons, 1969. Although the title of this work suggests a specific interest in form criticism, this valuable study covers all areas of analysis, including that of tradition history. Available in paperback edition in the series Scribner Studies in Biblical Interpretation.

PROBLEMS OF TRANSMISSION

ALBRIGHT, WILLIAM F. *Yahweh and the Gods of Canaan: A Historical Analysis of Two Contrasting Faiths.* Garden City: Doubleday & Co., 1968. This book develops further many of Albright's viewpoints on the religion of Israel. Of particular value are his frequent discussions of the nature and formation of Old Testament literature in the light of ancient Near Eastern discoveries, including oral tradition.

NIELSEN, EDUARD. *Oral Tradition: A Modern Problem in Old Testament Introduction.* Studies in Biblical Theology, no. 11. Naperville, Ill.: Alec R. Allenson, 1954. Offers a thoroughgoing application of oral tradition to the study of several Old Testament sections.

Rigid Scrutiny, A. Critical essays of Ivan Engnell translated by John T. Willis. Nashville: Vanderbilt University Press, 1969. A collection of selected articles illustrating the novel approach of the Scandinavian tradition historian. Especially pertinent to matters discussed in this book are Chapters 1 and 6.

THE FORMATION OF TRADITION

CHILDS, BREVARD S. *Memory and Tradition in Israel.* Studies in Biblical Theology, no. 37. Naperville, Ill.: Alec. R. Allenson, 1962. A study of the dynamics of Israel's memory through the vocabulary and texts of the Old Testament. Provides some original insights into how memory worked to shape essentials in Israel's faith and understanding.

MOWINCKEL, SIGMUND. *The Psalms in Israel's Worship.* Translated by D. R. Ap-Thomas. 2 vols. New York: Abingdon Press, 1962. One of Mowinckel's well-known studies of the psalms, incorporating his view on the cult and traditions behind the psalms.

VON RAD, GERHARD. *Moses.* New York: Association Press, 1960. A small paperback study written in popular style, giving the assessment of the figure of Moses in the Old Testament by this famous tradition historian.

THE BOOK OF GENESIS

GUNKEL, HERMANN. *The Legends of Genesis: The Biblical Saga and History.* Translated by W. H. Carruth. New York: Schocken Books, 1964. Contains a translation of Gunkel's introduction to his German commentary on Genesis.

NOTH, MARTIN. *Überlieferungsgeschichte des Pentateuch.* Stuttgart: W. Kohlhammer Verlag, 1948. Noth's pioneering literary and traditio-historical analysis of the Pentateuch.

VON RAD, GERHARD. *Genesis.* Translated by John H. Marks. Philadelphia: Westminster Press, 1961. An important commentary using literary critical, form critical, and traditio-historical analysis.

THE PROPHETS

BIRKELAND, HARRIS. *Zum hebräischen Traditionswesen.* Oslo: Jacob Dybwad, 1958. A significant monograph on the role of oral tradition in the formation of the prophetic books.

GUNNEWEG, A. H. J. *Mündliche und schriftliche Tradition der vorexilischen Prophetenbücher als Problem der neueren Pro-*

phetenforschung. Göttingen: Vandenhoeck & Ruprecht, 1959. A critical analysis of the place and limitations of oral tradition in interpreting the prophetic books.

MOWINCKEL, SIGMUND. *Prophecy and Tradition.* Oslo: Jacob Dybwad, 1946. Develops the idea of the prophets as primarily preachers, whose words were carried along and given shape by circles of disciples.

TRADITION HISTORY AND THEOLOGY

VON RAD, GERHARD. *Old Testament Theology.* Translated by D. M. G. Stalker. 2 vols. New York: Harper & Row, 1962, 1965. A significant study in Old Testament theology, utilizing the results of traditio-historical research throughout.

WESTERMANN, CLAUS, ed. *Essays on Old Testament Hermeneutics.* Richmond: John Knox Press, 1963. This volume presents translated essays, most of which appeared in various German journals. Many of them indicate the new problems for a Christian understanding of the Old Testament opened up through recent Old Testament study, including traditio-historical contributions.